D1639469

ENGLISH
ROMANESQUE
ARCHITECTURE

REPTON, DERBYSHIRE, CRYPT

10th century

ENGLISH ROMANESQUE ARCHITECTURE
BEFORE THE CONQUEST

By A. W. CLAPHAM, F.S.A.

OXFORD
AT THE CLARENDON PRESS

Oxford University Press, Amen House, London E.C.4

GLASGOW NEW YORK TORONTO MELBOURNE WELLINGTON
BOMBAY CALCUTTA MADRAS KARACHI LAHORE DACCA
CAPE TOWN SALISBURY NAIROBI IBADAN ACCRA
KUALA LUMPUR HONG KONG

FIRST PUBLISHED 1930
REPRINTED LITHOGRAPHICALLY AT THE UNIVERSITY PRESS, OXFORD
FROM SHEETS OF THE FIRST EDITION
1964

PRINTED IN GREAT BRITAIN AT THE UNIVERSITY PRESS, OXFORD
BY VIVIAN RIDLER, PRINTER TO THE UNIVERSITY

PREFACE

A FEW words are perhaps necessary to explain the plan and purpose on and with which the following pages were written. The Romanesque period in English Architecture has nearly always been treated as an introductory chapter to the study of Gothic art, and as such has been commonly viewed as a mine, in which the modern writer has sought for the origins of the style which was his chief concern. As an essay in construction or as an expression of beauty in form and decoration the early Gothic style deserves its pre-eminence, but like all perfect things it falls short in its appeal. The human mind craves, even in its architecture, some reflection of human imperfection, and the latent historical sense requires an art which mirrors the life and thoughts of its creators. Thus, however well the flower of French Gothic may illustrate the age of St. Louis, the equally pure contemporary English style is no illustration of the feeble English King or of his distracted country. It exemplifies not only a form of internationalization in art—this had been in a measure accomplished in earlier periods —but a power of selection which, while it showed a higher technical development, inevitably produced a certain lack of variety. The emergence of this power of selection appears to have coincided with the growing importance of the architect as opposed to the craftsman, and men such as William of Sens, Jean d'Orbais, Villard d'Honnecourt, and their fellows produced a certain uniformity in architecture in which such contending or concurrent influences as those of Cluny and Cîteaux, of Burgundy, Normandy, or Touraine can, generally speaking, be no longer traced.

With Romanesque building we are on a lower but more intimate and companionable plane; its expression, while both rich and varied, is marked by all those frailties and imperfections which are the proper symptoms of a pro-

gressive art, and illustrate so vividly the mind of its authors
and the age which gave it birth. Thus the main periods of
English Romanesque, each in their turn, form a fitting
expression of the political, social, and intellectual status of
the nation, and exemplify the strength and weakness of
Saxon and Norman alike.

The first two periods of this English Romanesque are
alone dealt with in the present volume, bringing the story
down to the Norman Conquest. It has been my endeavour
to produce a consecutive and logical account of the period,
and in pursuit of this object I have not hesitated to fill the
gaps in the story by theories of my own which may or may
not be substantiated by subsequent research. In doing this,
however, I have been at pains always to distinguish between fact and theory, so that the reader may know what
he may reject if he will. I have furthermore endeavoured
not to obscure the issue by too great a cloud of examples or
by lengthy descriptions of individual objects; in place of the
latter I have left the illustrations to speak for themselves,
wherever possible, having realized by bitter experience that
one illustration is worth many pages of type.

As some excuse for offering such a treatise to the public
I may urge that the subject has not before been treated as a
whole; for while Professor Baldwin Brown has dealt ex-
haustively with the architecture of the period and Professor
Brøndsted, Mr. W. G. Collingwood, and others with the
decoration, a general survey of both combined has not so
far been attempted. I cannot express too warmly my in-
debtedness to the writers above mentioned. The frequent
reference to their works in the footnotes is but a small
indication of my debt to them; and if my gleanings in fields
which are pre-eminently theirs have added anything to the
understanding of the subject the major part of the credit
must be assigned to those who have so ably shown the way.

I must furthermore express my great obligation to my
friends Mr. C. R. Peers, C.B.E., P.S.A., and to Mr. G. McN.

Rushforth, F.S.A., for having read the proofs of this volume and for many suggestions and corrections which have added materially to its value and accuracy.

My acknowledgements are also due to Dr. J. Bilson, F.S.A., for the use of his plan of Barton-on-Humber; to Mr. S. Toy, F.S.A., for the use of his plan of Brixworth; to Mr. W. H. Knowles, F.S.A., for permission to reproduce his plans of Deerhurst and Deerhurst Chapel; to Professor Baldwin Brown and others for similar permission; to Miss V. M. Dallas for drawing the plan of Glastonbury Abbey, and to Dr. F. J. Allen, Dr. L. Cobbett, Mr. E. Yates, Mr. F. K. Hirst, Mr. G. E. Chambers, and others for generously allowing me the use of the photographs here reproduced which bear their names. I am furthermore deeply indebted to Miss Dallas for compiling the index to this volume.

At the foot of each illustration I have added the date which I assign to each example, to avoid what may be the tiresome necessity of searching for such information in the text.

One last point must be noted. The spelling of Saxon proper names has always been a stumbling-block to any but the Anglo-Saxon scholar. As I have no pretensions to this title, I have, in general, adopted the form and spelling which appeared to me the most familiar to the general reader, with less regard to its philological correctness than to its popular acceptance. This course may be a sacrifice of accuracy to expediency, but those who know will not be deceived, while those who know not will not be confused.

A. W. C.

July, 1930.

CONTENTS

LIST OF FIGURES IN THE TEXT

LIST OF PLATES

Chapter I

INTRODUCTORY

THE intermittent persecution to which the early Christian Church was subject, from the time of Nero to that of Diocletian, was obviously unfavourable to the building of any edifice for the public celebration of the rites of the Church. From the time of Trajan suppressive edicts were continuously existent, but there were yet periods of greater or less duration when these edicts were not enforced; even in times of persecution their severity or even effectiveness was largely dependent on the temper of the governors of the individual provinces. It follows that, though the persecution might rage in Rome, the Church in the remoter provinces might yet enjoy comparative peace.[1]

The places of Christian reunion in Apostolic and sub-Apostolic times would seem to have been generally the private houses of the richer and more important converts; and this practice would serve well enough while the Church was in its infancy, or while persecution rendered the assembly of a numerous body in one place both impolitic and hazardous. The chapels in the Roman catacombs served equally well for small and secret meetings, and furthermore had a certain legal status as the property of the funerary colleges. It is obvious, however, that as the Church increased in numbers, and its members from time to time enjoyed a modified toleration, such practices must have given place to a more ordered system, and buildings capable of accommodating a larger congregation must have been erected. The earliest literary evidence of a church, properly so called, relates to Arbela in Mesopotamia,[2] where

[1] There were, furthermore, countries lying to the east of the Empire where Christianity enjoyed almost entire immunity from persecution and where, consequently, its development was unfettered.

[2] J. Strzygowski, *Origin of Christian Church Art* (1923), p. 25.

B

a church was built by Isaac, third bishop of the city (123–
36); the chronicle recording this fact dates only from the
sixth century, but there is no reason to doubt the statement
as the building still survived at that date. Another mention
appears in the Chronicle of Edessa,[1] which describes the
destruction of a church there by an inundation in 202. This
notice implies the existence of the building for some time
before the event narrated, and it is evident that, on the
eastern borders of the Empire and beyond, the building of
churches was suffered long before such a practice was permitted at Rome. It is, however, not long after this later
date that Lampridius[2] records the action of Alexander
Severus, about 222, in deciding in favour of the Christians
who desired to build a church on land in Rome claimed by
the tavern-keepers.

It is in any case certain that during the comparatively
long interval of peace between the edict of toleration of
Gallienus (260) and the last persecution under Diocletian
(303), a large number of churches were built throughout the
Empire; but, except for casual references to their existence
such as that in Eusebius, no further information as to their
size and form is available from any literary source. It is
curious also that with one exception no recognizable trace
of any public church of this period has yet come to light,
and the particulars of the one exception perhaps provide an
explanation of this lack. The foundations and pavement of
the church in question (Fig. 1) were uncovered in 1895 and
1900 at Parenzo[3] in Istria, and, though several authors have
thrown doubts on the pre-Diocletian date of the structure,
both its form and the subsequent architectural history of the
site render the early attribution almost a certainty. The existing cathedral of Parenzo was built by Bishop Euphrasius

---

[1] *Bib. orient. Chron. d'Édesse*, chap. viii, pp. 390–1.
[2] *Hist. Aug. Script.*, Alexander Severus, chap. xlix.
[3] See O. Marucchi in *Nuovo Bull. di Archeologia Christiana* (1896), pp. 14 and
122. A somewhat similar building, with parallel naves, has been found at
Zenica, Herzegovina; see R. Munro, *Rambles in Bosnia* (1900), p. 350.

before 543, as is attested by an inscription in mosaic relating to its endowment; and there is nothing in the architecture or decoration of the church to throw doubt on the statement. This cathedral overlies the walls and pavements of an earlier cathedral of similar plan but smaller dimensions, which has been assigned with every appearance of probability to the Constantinian age. Immediately to the north, and partly underlying both these cathedrals, was a yet earlier structure of much smaller dimensions than either of its successors, which had been destroyed by fire. This structure was a simple rectangle (75½ ft. by 26 ft.) to which a second building of similar form and size was added on the south side. The floors were covered with mosaic pavement containing the names of certain donors, and at

PARENZO
Early church

FIG. 1.

the east end of the northern half were remains of the posts of the canopy over the altar or of the altar itself. The walls were of slight construction and show no trace of architectural ornament. Such is the building which in all probability was erected by the Christians of Parenzo during, or not long before, the reign of Diocletian, and was destroyed in the persecution of 303-4. Compared with the cathedrals of the fourth and fifth centuries its simplicity of plan and absence of ornament are most striking, and it is precisely the type of modest and unpretentious structure that might be expected from the uncertain tolerance of the Imperial authorities on the one hand and the semi-apologetic daring of the nonconformist body on the other. The Act of Toleration of 1689 in this country produced a very similar type of building in England, and the form and character of the church at Parenzo is indeed the best evidence of the date of its erection. It may well be that this very lack of character is the reason why no other churches of the pre-Constantinian age have been identified; for it is not often that the pavement alone will supply sufficient evidence to identify the purpose of the building which contains it. It may readily be believed that a large number, if not the majority, of these early churches followed the type of Parenzo; but this does not necessarily imply that no churches on a larger and more elaborate plan were erected.

The evidence, however, is lacking to determine if any of the churches of the pre-Constantinian age contained the germ from which was developed the church-plan adopted at Rome immediately after the Peace of the Church. This plan would almost appear to have sprung to birth fully formed, for there is a uniformity in the arrangement of the Constantinian churches which argues the adoption of some standard type by the Imperial architects of that age. Constantine himself built extensively at Rome, Jerusalem, Antioch, and Constantinople, and his example was followed by the Imperial family and by bishops and governors of provinces throughout the Empire. Setting aside, for the moment, churches of the circular or central type of plan which were the result of special conditions and perhaps of Eastern origin, the whole corpus of Constantinian church-building exhibits few variations. The church was a rectangular building with a clearstorey and side aisles, roofed in timber and terminated at one end in a vaulted apse, which was preceded in the larger churches by a transept. In front of the entrance was a rectangular court or atrium, with covered corridors or galleries along the four sides, which in smaller churches were reduced to a single gallery or narthex against the front of the church. The origin of this type of church-plan, generally termed basilican, has been the subject of prolonged discussion and analysis, which in the end has left the subject very much in the same position as it was at the outset. The old theory that pagan and secular buildings were handed over to the Christians for transformation into churches has long been exploded, and hardly a single instance of such a practice can be proved until a far later date. It has been pointed out by the late M. de Lasteyrie that there was no standard plan for the secular Roman basilica,[1] and when, in occasional instances, this plan equates with that of the early Christian church, such an equation is purely fortuitous. The same objections apply with even more force to the theory deriving the church-plan from that of the Roman house, which derives almost its sole support from the presence of the atrium in both types of buildings, and is otherwise too fantastic to deserve serious consideration. The whole discussion, as M. Enlart has pointed out, is really beside the mark; the problem confronting the Constantinian architects was to all intents and purposes a new one, and a type of building was evolved to meet all the various requirements of the Christian rite, and not necessarily based on any pre-existing model any more than the modern railway terminus is based on the plan of a market-hall or a swimming-bath.

This, however, does not imply that similar circumstances had not produced a similar result before the age of Constantine, and this is exemplified by the discovery of the Porta Maggiore Basilica at Rome in 1917.[2] This little subterranean building (Fig. 2) reproduces all the essential features of the basilican church; it consists of a nave of three bays with aisles, an apse at the east end, and a small atrium at the west end through which the building is entered. The building has been dated, on technical grounds, to about the middle of the first century A.D., and was erected as a place of worship for one of the numerous mystery-cults then

[1] R. de Lasteyrie, *L'architecture religieuse en France à l'époque Romane*, p. 48. The subject has recently been reconsidered by L. Bréhier in the *Bulletin Monumental* (1927), p. 221, following on the researches of the late G. Leroux (*Les origines de l'édifice hypostyle en Grèce, en Orient et chez les Romains*, 1913). These authors distinguish two types of civil basilicas in use by the Romans—the Oriental and the Greek—and derive the Christian basilica from the Greek type.
[2] See J. Carcopino, *La basilique pythagoricienne de la Porte Majeure*, Paris, 1927.

prevalent in Rome, which reacted in no small degree on the early Christian Church. The precise nature of this cult is unknown, but its aims and aspirations are indicated by a series of stucco reliefs on the walls and vault. The needs of the cult evidently demanded precisely the same type of structure as those of the Christian church, and it may be

PORTA MAGGIORE BASILICA

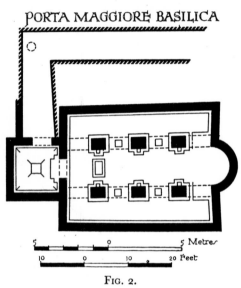

FIG. 2.

supposed that the initiates occupied the building itself and the uninitiated the atrium, just as the baptized Christians and the catechumens occupied the corresponding portions of the Christian church. The main distinction between the two types of building is entirely ritual, what may have been the altar of the Porta Maggiore Basilica being towards the west end of the building; there are, however, traces of a ritual enclosure in front of the apse, corresponding to the cancellum of the Christian church and a cathedra within it.[1]

The most important surviving churches of the basilican type and of the age of Constantine and his immediate suc-

---

[1] A parallel development of the same type is to be found in the third-century Synagogue at Hammân-Lif, near Carthage, with atrium, vestibule, and hall ending in a semicircular niche. *Revue Archéologique*, 1884 (first half), p. 273.

cessors are to be found in Rome, Africa, and Syria, and of these a considerable number were the work of Constantine himself and his mother Helena. The largest of his churches, St. Peter's at Rome (Fig. 3), was destroyed in the fifteenth and sixteenth centuries to make way for the present building, but its plan and form are preserved in drawings of that age. The church of St. John Lateran survives in a much altered state, as does the church of St. Laurence-without-the-Walls and a number of other Roman churches. The plans of several more have been recovered by excavation, so that the general features of the Italian churches of that period are well established. The same remark applies to Palestine, where remains of most of the Constantinian churches have come to light, and one of them—the church of the Nativity at Bethlehem—survives largely intact. In Africa but few of the churches can be definitely dated to this period, but the type there remains fairly constant through the next century. The main features of the churches of the basilican type have already been touched upon; and, in the three districts referred to, the type is little varied. The distinguishing features of the Italian buildings are (a) the transept, separated from the nave by the 'arch of triumph', roofed at right angles to the main body, and having a single apse, and (b) the atrium. The transept is present at St. Peter's, St. John Lateran, St. Mary Major, and numerous later Roman churches, but seems to have found little favour in Africa or the East. The atrium is an almost invariable adjunct to the early Roman churches, but is only present in the more important churches of Africa or Palestine. The simple basilican type of building without transept is common to all three districts, and at this period is generally accompanied by two or more chambers flanking the east end of the building. Architecturally the buildings, generally, are severely plain, depending for their effect mainly on marble casing, mosaic, or other applied decoration. The aisles are separated from the nave by colonnades supporting,

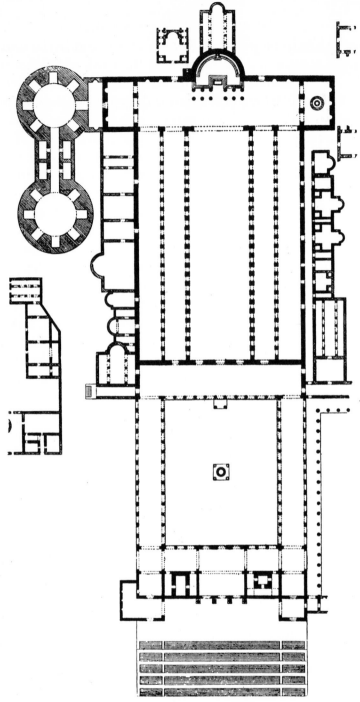

FIG. 3. Old St. Peter's, Rome. (Scale 116 ft. to 1 in.)

in the earliest churches, flat entablatures of the true Classic tradition, which, however, very soon gave way to a series of arches. The windows are large openings generally arched, and the doors commonly square-headed. The roofs, except in the apse, are invariably of timber.

One other point must be noticed, as it has a direct bearing on the planning of the early churches in Britain. The Roman churches of the fourth century, and in all probability those of Italy in general, had the apse at the west end of the building, so that the celebrant standing behind the altar faced towards the east and towards the congregation.[1] The first church in Italy, so far as is known, that departed from this tradition and had the apse at the east end, was the cathedral of Ravenna, built between 370 and 397 and destroyed in the eighteenth century. Outside Italy the apse was more commonly placed at the east end than in the reverse position, and there are numerous examples of fourth-century churches in Syria and Africa, such as the church of the Nativity at Bethlehem and the basilica at Orléansville, which follow the normal arrangement.[2]

It is unfortunate that in the north-western provinces of the Roman Empire the architectural traces of early Christianity are exceedingly meagre. The foundations of one fourth-century church have come to light in southern Gaul and one in Britain; the foundations of S. Pierre at Vienne may also go back to this period, but the fourth-century portions of the cathedral at Trier are now considered to have formed part of the Imperial palace, and must consequently be subtracted from the scanty list. It is generally assumed by French archaeologists that Christianity penetrated into

[1] The practice was no doubt derived from the Roman temple, in which the portico normally faced the east.
[2] The researches of Strzygowski have proved the existence, at this period, of a group or groups of churches in the Parthian and Persian provinces, of a type totally distinct from the basilican; they had, however, little or no influence on the architecture of the western church until a far later date, and even then such influence was largely indirect.

C

northern Gaul at a comparatively late period, but if this be so the partial conversion of Britain must have preceded it, as there was certainly an organized Church here at the beginning of the fourth century, and the known existence of a church in the comparatively small city of Silchester argues the presence of one or more in each of the larger cities of the province.

But while the Christian sarcophagi [1] of southern Gaul testify to the existence of a numerous and flourishing church in that district, there is an entire absence of such evidence in Britain, where, apart from the church at Silchester, definite traces of Christianity are confined to a few portable objects and occasional symbols occurring in mosaic pavements. This paucity of evidence is in striking contrast to the numerous and often important traces of the opposition cult of Mithras and other eastern cults, which may perhaps imply that Christianity in Britain was largely confined to the poorer classes.

The three buildings mentioned above as representing the only surviving remains of fourth-century churches in Gaul and Britain deserve careful consideration; though it is quite impossible to base any general conclusions on so small a number of examples. The church (Fig. 4) at Lugdunum Convenarum [2] (S. Bertrand de Comminges) was excavated just before the Great War. The coins found on the site, and an inscription found near-by, leave little doubt that it was built in the first half of the fourth century; it was ruined by the Vandals in 409, subsequently restored, and finally destroyed by the Burgundians in 585. It was built on the site of an earlier domestic building and consisted of a nave

---

[1] Le Blant, *Les sarcophages Chrét. de la Gaule.*
[2] M. Dieulafoy, 'Basilique Constantinienne de Lugdunum Convenarum', in *Bull. Acad. des Inscriptions et Belles-Lettres* (1914), pp. 59 et seq. The plan there published is incorrect in several particulars, and subsequent excavations have revealed the square fore-court to the west of the nave. The plan reproduced below shows the discoveries down to the year 1927, and is compiled and corrected from notes taken on the spot.

(67 ft. by 40½ ft.) with a fore-court to the west and a deep chancel terminating in a three-sided apse. There was a double foundation to the apse, the two lines of walling following the same form but one being more stilted than the other. The inner apse was obviously a later reconstruction, perhaps after the earlier east end had been ruined. The church was paved with white marble squares and the walls were covered internally with a coating of

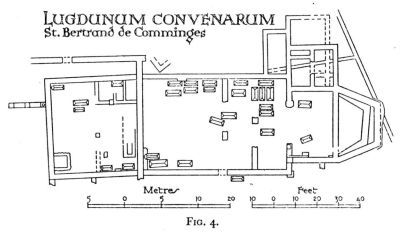

FIG. 4.

pink cement. In the opinion of M. Dieulafoy the walls could not have been carried up to any considerable height, and he supposes that arcades supported the timber-work of the roof; of these, however, there is no definite evidence. The apse is towards the south-east and consequently not in the Roman manner, and the form of the apse has no analogies in Italian churches of the same period, but may be paralleled in North Africa, though here the dating of the buildings is uncertain. The chancel appears to have been entered by a triple arcade of which the middle bay was wider than the side bays. This feature also can be paralleled in North Africa. It would appear, therefore, that the Pyrenees were more closely in touch with Africa and the East, perhaps via Spain and the ports of Provence, than with Italy and Rome.

It was, however, otherwise with the Rhone valley, if one may judge by the remains of the church of S. Pierre, Vienne.[1] It is now considered by M. Formigé that only the foundations of the outer walls and apse of the building date back to the beginning of the fifth century, but this is sufficient to show that it followed the normal lines of the smaller Roman churches, consisting of an aisled nave with a shallow central apse; it should, however, be noted that the apse is at the east end.

The small Christian church at Silchester (Fig. 5, 1) was excavated in 1892. It consisted of a nave terminating on the west in an apse, aisles flanking the nave and having projections at the west end in the form of transepts, and a narthex across the front opposite the apse. The walls had not survived to a sufficient height to show whether the aisles were separated from the nave by arcades or by a solid wall pierced by openings. The church was paved with coarse red tesserae, but in front of the chord of the apse was a square of checker-work mosaic surrounded by a band of lozenges. This supposedly marks the position of the wooden altar, but the pavement is worn on the east side of this square instead of the west, which would be the normal position for the celebrant at an altar in the western or Roman position. The transeptal projections appear to have served the purpose of a prothesis and a diaconicon—the former, on the south, being approached from the aisle, and the latter, on the north, being approached from the chancel. The purpose of these chambers, which are more normal to the eastern than to the western church, will be further considered in connexion with the seventh-century churches of Kent. A short distance to the east of the Silchester church was a square foundation supposed to have supported the laver where the faithful washed before entering the church. No evidence of the date of the building was afforded by the excavations, but it may be assumed to belong to the fourth century. The plan of the church would

[1] J. Formigé in *Congrès Arch. de France* (Valence, 1923), p. 77.

seem to reflect the Roman type with a transept, and this accords well with the west position of the apse, but the

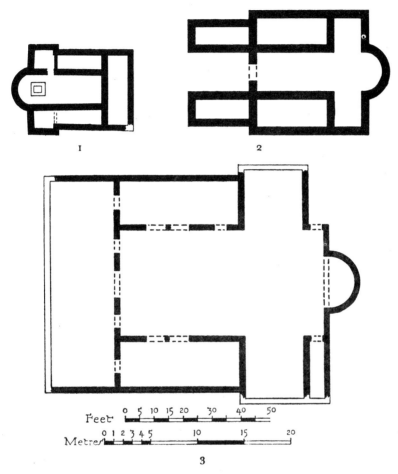

FIG. 5. 1. Silchester; 2. Jatagan; 3. Como, SS. Peter and Paul.

whole building is on so minute a scale that comparison with much larger buildings may well be misleading. There are, however, remains of two other churches of almost exactly similar plan, and of not much greater dimensions, as far apart as North Italy and Armenia. The former at Como [1] (Fig. 5, 3) was founded by St. Abundius about 490;

[1] See plan in Dartein, *Étude sur l'architecture Lombarde*, text p. 313, plan Pl. 75.

the latter at Jatagan,[1] Begetjö Kosu (Fig. 5, 2), is not closely dated. It would thus seem that this type of plan for small churches was very widely distributed.

A second possible example of an early Christian church in this country has recently come to light during the excavations at Caerwent (Monmouthshire). Adjoining the road, in the insula immediately south of the forum, remains were discovered of a small rectangular building, 22½ ft. by 17¼ ft., with a shallow apse in the east wall and traces of what may have been a large narthex at the west end. The building was of rough construction, and belonged to the very latest phase of the Roman period, if, indeed, it was not a work of the immediately succeeding age. The layer of earth and rubbish which intervened between it and the important Roman structure on a corner of which it stood showed that this earlier building must have been demolished and have lain waste before the erection of the supposed church. I am indebted for this information to Dr. R. E. M. Wheeler, who superintended the excavations.

Before leaving the subject of Romano-British churches it may be noted that Bede, and no doubt his informant, believed that St. Augustine on his arrival at Canterbury in 598 found there remains of two churches of this period, one within and one without the Roman walls. There is no reason to doubt the story, but it is very unlikely that after two centuries of neglect and destruction any considerable part of them could be patched up and restored to use. In any case there are now no traces of Roman work at St. Martin's, and if any survived at the cathedral they were swept away by Lanfranc in the eleventh century.[2]

Between the end of the fourth century and the coming of St. Augustine the evidences of Christianity in Britain are confined to Wales, Cornwall, and Galloway. They consist

---

[1] See plan in J. Strzygowski, *Kleinasien* (1903), p. 55.
[2] Eddius implies that St. Wilfrid made use of the consecrated places abandoned by the British in Northumbria (*Vita Wilfridi*, chap. xvii).

of a considerable number of inscriptions in barbarous Latin which can only be approximately dated by the degree of their barbarity in language or lettering. One example in Wales, some half a dozen in Cornwall, and three in Galloway bear the XP monogram. These last may be dated to near the period of St. Ninian's mission *c.* 400, but of the church of stone built by him at Whithorn no traces have yet come to light.

Chapter II

CHURCH BUILDING UNDER THE HEPTARCHY

THE conversion of England begun by St. Augustine and his Roman mission occurred at a time when southern Europe and especially Italy was again in the melting-pot. The tide of Justinian's conquests had ebbed, the Lombards had overrun the country, a series of disasters both natural and artificial had overtaken the people, and to this was shortly to be added the arrival of a host of refugees from Africa, Egypt, and Syria, displaced by the Moslem conquests. The result of these factors, the last excepted, on Italian art and architecture was deplorable; and Signor Cattaneo [1] has shown how rapidly the art of sixth-century Italy disappeared in the seventh, and by what slow and painful steps it gradually revived. It was from this rapidly decaying society that St. Augustine's mission came, and it may be to the unfortunate condition of Italy that the brilliant art of later seventh-century England is to some extent due, for the condition of this country, at any rate after the coming of Theodore in 669, offered a more tempting asylum for the dispossessed Greek or the harried Italian than any other available state. The Anglo-Saxon too was in the first fervour of his conversion, and kings and people welcomed any stranger who, whether ecclesiastic or artist, could teach them to acquire the new learning, to practise the new rites, or to build in the new manner. This is abundantly evident from the pages of Bede, and the resultant art of seventh- and eighth-century England illustrates by its very complexity the widely different sources from which it was derived.

English church-building of the first period—the seventh century—is sharply divided between the south and the

[1] R. Cattaneo, *Architecture in Italy from the Sixth to the Eleventh Century* (1896), pp. 23–5.

north, the southern or Kentish type of building being due to the Roman mission of St. Augustine, and the northern or Northumbrian type to the masons introduced by Benedict Biscop and Wilfrid. The Irish missionaries to whom the conversion of the north was primarily due can have had little or no permanent effect on the architecture of the district, as at this period they were builders in wood or at best in dry-stone walling.

The Kentish Group

The seventh-century churches of south-east England form a remarkably homogeneous group [1] with methods of construction, plan, and arrangement so uniform that without the aid of any literary evidence it would be obvious that they belong to one age and are the product of the same stage of culture. Fortunately literary evidence enables an exact date to be given to nearly all of these buildings, and the result is a series of nearly contemporary examples which it would be difficult if not impossible to parallel elsewhere in Europe at so remote a date.

The group consists of six churches of which the plans have been more or less completely recovered, and the remains of two more, one of which is a mere fragment and one a somewhat enigmatic structure of a character rather apart from the rest. The surviving details of each building will first be considered, after which some attempt will be made to explain their peculiarities and to indicate the sources from which these peculiarities were drawn. The buildings of the same type will be dealt with, so far as possible, chronologically, as follows:

1. Canterbury, SS. Peter and Paul.
2. Canterbury, St. Mary.
3. Canterbury, St. Pancras.
4. Rochester, St. Andrew
5. Lyminge, St. Mary
6. Bradwell, St. Peter.
7. Reculver, St. Mary.

[1] See C. R. Peers, 'On Saxon Churches of the St. Pancras Type', *Arch. Journ.*, lviii (1902), pp. 402–34; and G. Baldwin Brown, *The Arts in Early England*, Architecture (1925), chap. iv.

1. SS. Peter and Paul, Canterbury [1] (Fig. 6), was founded
as the chief church of an abbey by St. Augustine in 597, and
was still unfinished at his death in 604. The excavations
conducted on the site between the years 1904 and 1924
have uncovered all that still remains of this building, and

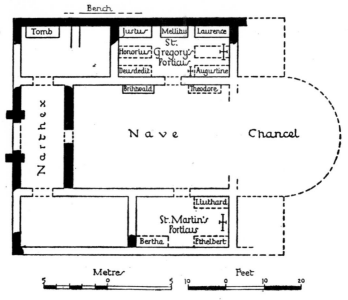

Fig. 6.   Canterbury, SS. Peter and Paul.

the fairly complete plan, lacking the east end, is the result.
The body of the church was 27 ft. wide and had a narthex
11 ft. wide across its west end. It was flanked on either side
by porticus or chapels 12 ft. wide, those on the north still
containing tombs. The literary evidence supplies the facts
that the north-east porticus was dedicated to St. Gregory
and contained the tombs of St. Augustine and his immediate
successors in the See of Canterbury, and that the south-
east porticus contained the tombs of King Ethelbert,
Bertha his wife, and others. The surviving tomb in the
north-west porticus is nameless. Two tombs in the body

---

[1] C. R. Peers and A. W. Clapham, 'St. Augustine's Abbey Church, Canterbury, before the Norman Conquest', *Archaeologia*, lxxvii, p. 201.

PLATE 1

ST. PANCRAS, CANTERBURY, W. PORCH AND NAVE

c. 600

of the church adjoining the porticus of St. Gregory contained the bodies of St. Theodore and Brihtwald, archbishops. The eastern termination of the church was entirely destroyed, but the northern wall of St. Gregory's porticus continued a sufficient distance eastwards to show that some other portion of the church adjoined the porticus on the east. The side walls of the body of the church were also destroyed, but the literary evidence, by speaking of a doorway opening into St. Gregory's porticus, shows that walls and not an arcade separated the porticus from the body of the church. The walls are almost entirely of Roman brick, 2 ft. thick, and have square buttresses flanking the western entrance. The floor was laid throughout with a pavement of *opus signinum* (cement with pounded brick) of such hardness that it had suffered but little after a lapse of 1,300 years. Remains of a bench were found outside the north wall of the building, and it was evident that the external face of the wall was plastered.

2. St. Mary, Canterbury[1] (Fig. 49), was founded about 620 by Edbald, King of Kent, and stood a few yards east of the church just described. It has been entirely destroyed with the exception of the west wall, which indicated a building of the internal width of 22½ ft. with a central doorway having a shallow external rebate on each jamb. The literary evidence shows that when the west end was pulled down by Abbot Wulfric about 1057 it was surrounded by porticus. The surviving wall is of Roman brick.

3. St. Pancras, Canterbury[2] (Fig. 7), still standing in ruins about 260 ft. east of the church of St. Mary, is first mentioned in the late fourteenth-century chronicle of William Thorne who connects it with St. Augustine. Its character, however, so exactly conforms to that of the churches already described that there can be no doubt as to its date. As first

[1] *Archaeologia*, lxxvii, p. 211.
[2] *Archaeologia Cantiana*, xxv, pp. 222–37; W. H. St. J. Hope, *The Chapel of St. Pancras*.

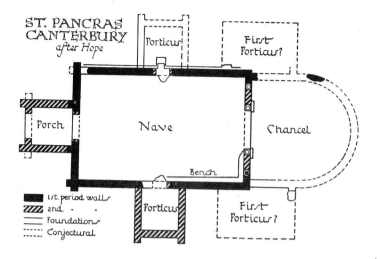

ST. PANCRAS
CANTERBURY
after Hope

Porticus

First
Porticus?

Porch

Nave

Chancel

Bench

First
Porticus?

1st. period walls
2nd. " "
Foundations
Conjectural

Porticus

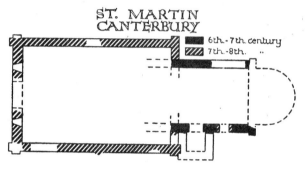

ST. MARTIN
CANTERBURY

6th.-7th. century
7th.-8th. "

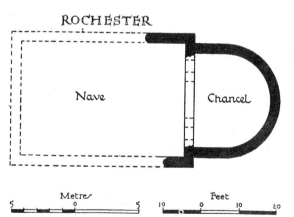

ROCHESTER

Nave

Chancel

Metres
5   0   5

Feet
10   0   10   20

FIG. 7.

N,B. The scales are the same for all three plans.

planned it consisted of a nave, 42½ ft. by 26½ ft., and a chancel formed of a stilted apse and separated from the nave by an arcade of three arches resting on stone columns. Foundations of some significance were found, in the excavations of 1900, projecting from the south side of the chancel and from the north side of the nave near its east end, also of a buttress about the middle of the north wall of the nave. While the building was in course of erection a west porch was added to the pair of buttresses against the west wall, and probably at the same time a porticus was added in the middle of each side of the nave and the side arches opening into the chancel were blocked. The walls are still partly standing, one wall of the west porch (Pl. 1) surviving to some height; these walls are 1 ft. 10 in. in thickness and are built almost entirely of Roman brick. The surviving remains of the apse were so small that it is uncertain if the external face was curved or polygonal.

4. St. Andrew, Rochester[1] (Fig. 7), was founded by King Ethelbert in 604, and the remains of the church uncovered in 1889 accord so closely with the form of the Canterbury churches as to leave little doubt that they are the remains of the building in question. Little but rubble foundations survived, indicating a building 52 ft. by 28 ft. with an elliptical apse and a sleeper-wall across its entrance, probably to carry a triple arcade similar to that at St. Pancras. The circumstances attending the excavations were such as to leave it uncertain what adjuncts the church possessed to the north, south, and west.

5. St. Mary, Lyminge[2] (Fig. 8), was founded by St. Ethelburga soon after 633. The surviving remains, excavated about 1875, show the foundations of an apse separated from the body of the church by a triple arcade. There are some indications of a doorway at the west end of the north wall of the apse, opening into a porticus overlapping the apse

---

[1] *Archaeologia Cantiana*, xviii, p. 264, and xxiii, p. 212.
[2] *Ibid.*, x, p. cii, and *Arch. Journ.*, lviii, p. 419.

and nave on this side, and now mostly covered by the later church. The walls are of Roman brick and rubble.

6. St. Peter, Bradwell on Sea[1] (Fig. 8), is, with little doubt, to be identified with the church built at Ythancester by St. Cedd after 653. With the exception of its apse and porticus it is still standing (Pl. 2), and consisted of a nave 49½ ft. by 21½ ft. with an apse of the same width entered by a triple arcade. Remains of the west walls of both porticus survive—that on the north entered by a doorway just east of the arcade and that on the south by a doorway west of the arcade. The walls are mostly of re-used Roman stone-work and are supported by regularly spaced buttresses of considerable projection. The plain square windows are largely original, as is the wide west doorway which was apparently covered by a west porch. The triple arcade has been mostly destroyed, but portions of the side arches remain.

7. St. Mary, Reculver[2] (Fig. 8), is dated by an entry in the *Anglo-Saxon Chronicle* under 669 to the effect that King Egbert of Kent gave Reculver to Bassa, his mass-priest, to build a minster there. The remains of this church, pulled down in 1805, were uncovered in 1926–7. As originally planned it consisted of a nave 37½ ft. by 24 ft. with an apsidal chancel round within and polygonal without and entered by a triple arcade (Pl. 3) resting on two stone columns. A pair of porticus overlapping chancel and nave were entered by doorways east of the arcade. At a date not very far removed from the original foundation a series of porticus were added against the remaining parts of the nave walls, including a west porch. The main walls of the original nave are 2 ft. 5 in. thick and those of the porticus 2 ft. thick; they are built of Roman brick and rubble and are provided with square buttresses. The windows are

---

[1] *Roy. Com. on Hist. Mons., Essex*, iv, p. 15.
[2] C. R. Peers, 'Reculver, its Saxon Church and Cross', in *Archaeologia*, lxxvii, p. 241.

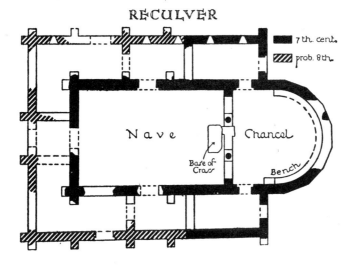

RECULVER

7th. cent.

prob. 8th.

Nave

Chancel

Base of
Cross

Bench

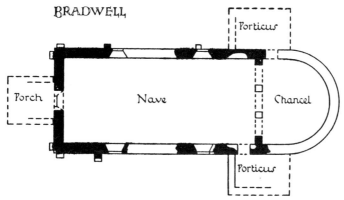

BRADWELL

Porticus

Porch

Nave

Chancel

Porticus

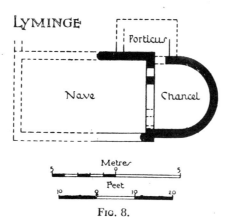

LYMINGE

Porticus

Nave

Chancel

Metres

Feet

FIG. 8.

splayed internally and had arched heads. The original doorways had shallow rebates in the jambs,[1] and the original floor was covered with a pavement of *opus signinum*, of fine quality, which still largely survives. The added porticus had a pavement of similar character, but this has mostly perished. The two stone columns now preserved in the precincts of Canterbury Cathedral are almost certainly of the period of the church, as their decoration differs entirely from Romano-British work. The capitals have a semi-classical architrave section, and the moulded bases are enriched with cable and raised key-pattern.

The eighth and last building of the group assignable to this period is the church of St. Martin at Canterbury[2] (Fig. 7), which does not conform to the rest of the series. The only part of the earliest church which survives is the chancel; but neither the form of its east end, nor its extent to the west, has yet been ascertained; it has certain features which will be returned to later, and which may reflect the historical particulars recorded of its building. The walls are 2 ft. 2 in. thick and are largely of Roman brick, and projecting from the south side was a tiny porticus with a floor of *opus signinum*.

Before proceeding to an examination of the characteristics of these churches it will be well to recall the circumstances under which they were built. Almost all of them are the productions of a band of Italian missionaries with at best a somewhat precarious foothold in a foreign and still largely heathen country. Both Kent and Essex lapsed into idolatry after their first conversion, and the political circumstances of the Church in both counties were hardly favourable to building on an extensive scale, until Theodore had brought some order out of the preceding chaos. It

---

[1] The marks on the threshold indicated that these doorways were originally lined with stone or marble slabs and that the rebate was designed for that purpose. Similar marks were found on the threshold of the west doorway of the little chapel of St. John the Baptist west of St. Mary's chapel at Glastonbury.
[2] Canon C. F. Routledge, *St. Martin's, Canterbury* (1898).

PLATE 2

BRADWELL, ESSEX, CHURCH FROM NW.
c. 660

PLATE 3

RECULVER, KENT, CHANCEL-ARCHES DURING DEMOLITION
c. 670

must furthermore be remembered that there is no evidence for Saxon building in any other material than timber before the arrival of St. Augustine's mission, and consequently any building undertaken by that mission in any other material must have been the work of imported masons from either Gaul or Italy, and their number must have been small. It is not, therefore, surprising that the buildings under consideration, while insignificant in scale, exhibit a technical capacity of a relatively high order, and that the *opus signinum* flooring at Canterbury and Reculver or the brick walling of St. Pancras church are hardly surpassed in genuine Roman work.

A careful study of the plans of the seven churches described above reveals a number of well-marked characteristics which must be dealt with before any attempt can be made to trace their source or origin. It will be noted firstly that all the apses are stilted, the terminal curve being struck from a point well to the east of the chancel-arch. At Reculver the external face is definitely polygonal, and this form is again reproduced at Brixworth, which will be described hereafter.

It may be that this refinement was not introduced until after the middle of the seventh century, as it does not appear in the earlier churches.[1] Definite remains of the triple opening into the chancel survive at four out of the seven examples in the group, and it is not unlikely that it occurred also in the other three.

The general use of buttresses appears only in the later churches of Bradwell and Reculver; the use of this feature at SS. Peter and Paul and St. Pancras, Canterbury, being almost confined to the pairs flanking the west doors, which may have had an ornamental rather than a structural significance.

---

[1] Only the foundations of these apses have, however, survived and the superstructure may have followed the semi-polygonal form; the apse at Reculver rests on a foundation of semicircular form both within and without.

The most remarkable characteristic of the whole group, however, is the form and position of the porticus. Where only one pair is present, the two chambers were placed symmetrically on either side of the church and overlapping the chancel and nave. Remains of both still exist at Reculver and Bradwell, traces of the north porticus at Lyminge, and the remains of foundations, noted above, at St. Pancras seem to indicate that a similar arrangement was at any rate projected at that church, and perhaps superseded by the building of the later porticus flanking the nave. In view of the possible origin of these chambers the position of the doorways opening into them is of considerable significance. At Reculver they were both entered from the chancel; the north porticus at Lyminge was also, in all probability, entered from the chancel, but at Bradwell the north porticus was entered from the chancel and the south porticus from the nave. At the other two Canterbury churches this portion of the plan has not survived. The provision of chambers for the subsidiary purposes of the church and its services is a common feature of the great majority of fifth- and sixth-century churches in Syria and North Africa, and a range of such chambers has recently been discovered adjoining the fourth-century basilica at S. Bertrand de Comminges,[1] but it is a curious fact that in Rome and western Italy this practice was early abandoned. Indeed, St. Paulinus of Nola,[2] writing about 400, states that in his new basilica he had placed two small apses, to the left and right of the main apse, in the place of sacristies. This either became or had already become the common practice in Roman church-building. Two of these chambers had a definite use in the Eastern church and were known as the Diaconicon and the Prothesis, the former being for the use of the clergy and for the keeping of the sacred vessels, and the latter being used for the reception

[1] *Bull. Acad. des Inscriptions et Belles-Lettres* (1914), p. 59.
[2] Paulinus of Nola, *Ep.* xxxii, 13.

of the offerings of the faithful and their preparation for the altar. In theory, then, the diaconicon should be approached from the chancel, and the prothesis from the nave because the oblations were ceremonially carried round through the iconostasis; this arrangement is preserved in certain early churches in both Africa and Syria, and is reflected in the little Romano-British church at Silchester. The vast majority of churches, however, which are available for study in Syria and Africa are aisled structures where the

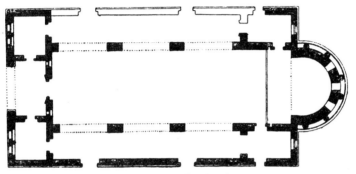

FIG. 9. Kalb Lauzeh. (Scale 1/400.)

diaconicon and prothesis take their place naturally as the prolongations of the two aisles, as at Kalb Lauzeh, Syria (Fig. 9). When it becomes necessary to adapt the same arrangement to an aisleless building it is obvious that the only possible position for the two chambers, if symmetry is to be preserved, is one overlapping the two main divisions of the church, so that one may be entered from the chancel and one from the nave. The theoretical arrangement in its entirety would appear to have been preserved at Bradwell; but in the other English instances, while the overlapping is retained, the strict arrangement of the doorways has been abandoned. It must of course be borne in mind that the original purpose of the two chambers had probably passed out of use in the Western church long before the advent of St. Augustine, and its retention in the plan points either to conservatism in its authors or to a more directly Eastern origin.

The other chambers adjoining the north and south walls of the naves at SS. Peter and Paul, Canterbury, and at Reculver, are of more certain purpose. The use of two of those at the first-named church as burial-places is proved from the beginning by the literary evidence.[1] In addition to this, it is recorded that St. Ethelburga was buried in a porticus on the north side of the church at Lyminge,[2] and that Tobias, Bishop of Rochester (693–726), was buried in a porticus, which he had made into a burial-place for himself, on the north side of that church.[3] It seems, therefore, reasonable to suppose that the added portions at Reculver served a like purpose. A further striking piece of evidence as to the use of these annexes is provided by a passage in one of the letters of St. Paulinus of Nola, in which he describes the new church of St. Felix at Nola, built *c.* 400. There were, he says, four 'cubicula' on each side of the nave, within the aisles, built for those who desired to pray or meditate on the word of God and for the sepulchral memorials of the departed; there were verses inscribed above the entrances.[4]

The western porticus no doubt always served as a porch or narthex, and the large size of the example at SS. Peter and Paul, Canterbury, may perhaps indicate that the early practice of separating the catechumens from the body of the church was not yet extinct in the time of S. Augustine's mission. In the later church at Reculver this feature has become a mere porch, and the same arrangement is preserved at Brixworth.

In the present state of knowledge of church architecture

---

[1] *Archaeologia*, lxvi, pp. 387 and 392, citing Bede, *Eccles. Hist.*, ii, chap. ii, and Goscelin, i, chap. xvii, &c.

[2] Goscelin, *Contra B. Mildrethae Usurpatores.* 'Eminentius et augustius monumentum in aquilionali porticu ad australem ecclesiae parietem arcu involutum.' The south wall of the early Norman church, here referred to, overlies the north porticus of the Saxon church.

[3] Bede, *Eccles. Hist.*, v, p. 23: 'Sepultus vero est in porticu sancti Pauli apostoli quam intra ecclesiam sancti Andreae sibi ipse in locum sepulchri fecerat.'

[4] Paulinus of Nola, *Ep.* xxxii, 12.

of the sixth and seventh centuries in western Europe it is
difficult to arrive at any definite conclusion as to the immediate source from which the builders of this group of
English churches drew their models. It is not too much to
say that in no other part of western Europe do there now
survive so many examples of a like age in so small a geographical compass. It is, indeed, the very paucity of available examples elsewhere which makes the problem at
present almost insoluble; and until chance or systematic
excavation brings to light the remains of the lesser churches
of the age in Italy, Gaul, and Germany the problem will
remain unsolved, for the great majority of known continental examples consist of buildings on a much larger
scale, which renders comparison more or less futile. Certain tentative conclusions may, however, be drawn from
the materials available; and amongst the most significant of these is the entire absence in Rome or Gaul of the
apse of the form and proportions of the English group.
Apses of the English proportions, however, occur in northern
Africa [1] and on the western Adriatic littoral; and the semi-
polygonal apses of Reculver and Brixworth are an obvious
copy of those of the sixth-century churches at Ravenna
or their prototypes [2] (Fig. 10, 1, 2). This form of apse, semicircular within and polygonal without, has long been
recognized as one evidence of the pronounced Byzantine
character of Ravennate architecture, for while this form is
a commonplace in the Eastern Empire it is hardly represented, outside England, in the western provinces at this
date. The triple arcade has generally been considered as
a symptom of the incapacity of the builders of the English
churches to erect an arch of wide span, such as would be
necessary if the triple arcade were dispensed with; it is,
however, very doubtful if this be the true explanation, for

---

[1] Cf. Biar el Kherba, Tigzirt (chapel), Annound, &c.
[2] Nearly all the early churches at Ravenna have or had apses of this form,
which is to be found also at Pomposa, Grado, Bagnacavallo, &c.

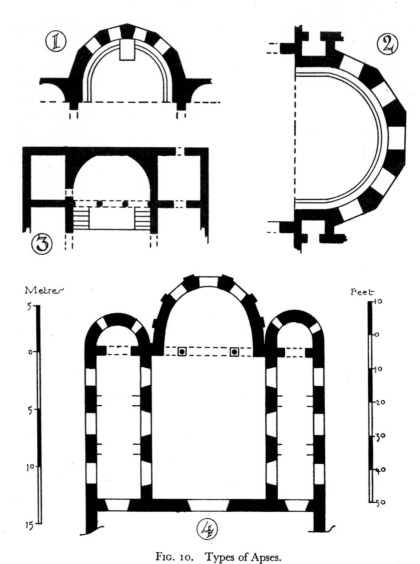

FIG. 10.   Types of Apses.

1. Parenzo, Cathedral, *c.* 530; 2. Ravenna, S. Apollinare in Classe, 534–49;
3. Bénian, Algeria, *c.* 440; 4. Parenzo, Episcopio, *c.* 530.

whether the builders came from Gaul, Italy, or farther afield, this construction would present no difficulties, and it is obvious that, whoever built these churches, it was not the native Saxon. Arcades of this character have, up to the present, been found in isolated (e.g. Lugdunum Convenarum, p. 11) examples in Europe and in the churches of North Africa, where there are a number of examples[1] (Fig. 10, 3), and where they seem to have fulfilled a double role, serving both as structural supports and as a form of iconostasis or screen. An interesting mosaic (Pl. 4) found near Tabarka[2] (Tunis) shows this feature in connexion with an aisled basilica, the greater span of the central arch being exactly reproduced at St. Pancras, Canterbury. The closest parallel, however, is to be found in the chapel of the Episcopio (*c.* 530) at Parenzo (Fig. 10, 4), where the triple arcade is accompanied by the curious elliptical apse, thought to have existed in some of the English examples.

The side-chambers or porticus of the English churches form the most distinctive feature of the plan, and the feature for which it is most difficult to find existing parallels. The purpose of the eastern pair of chambers has already been discussed, and is sufficiently represented in the aisled churches of North Africa and East Italy by chambers to the east of the aisles. The literary evidence, cited above, is conclusive as to the use and purpose of the chapels opening off the nave and may serve as some indication of their Italian origin. These adjuncts are, however, exceedingly rare outside this country. The church of SS. Peter and Paul of Como,[3] built by St. Abundius at the close of the fifth century, presents perhaps the closest analogy in Europe, for here there were no continuous arcades between the nave and its annexes, so that these can never have

---

[1] S. Gsell, *Les Monuments Antiques de l'Algérie*, ii, e.g. Bénian, p. 176; Tigzirt, p. 295; Tigzirt Chapel, p. 305, &c.

[2] Reproduced in *Mon. Piot*, vol. xiii, and hence O. Marucchi, *Éléments d'archéologie chrétienne* (2nd edit.), iii, 20.

[3] Dartein, *Étude sur l'architecture Lombarde*, p. 313.

formed a part of the main church. The large sixth-century aisled church at Salona [1] (Dalmatia) had an extra porticus or aisle on the north side, and perhaps also on the south side, which seem to have served for sepulchral purposes. The two early churches, the foundations of which have been discovered under the church of Romainmôtier [2] (Switzerland), have, both of them, square annexes adjoining the east end of the nave, but these have rather the appearance of sacristies, and the apse in each case is of the Roman form.

The narthex, of the form preserved at SS. Peter and Paul, Canterbury, is common to both the Eastern and Western churches at this period, and in Italy it often forms the east gallery of a rectangular atrium. Outside Italy the atrium forms an adjunct of only the larger churches in Syria and Africa, and not even of all of these. It dates from the earliest years of the Peace of the Church and continues through the Carolingian period. The only certain example of the atrium in England is that which existed at Winchester, where it was repaired in the tenth century, and so perhaps dated back to the seventh century. The narthex in the restricted form of a west porch, as exemplified at St. Pancras, Reculver, and Bradwell, had a far greater permanence, and it will be seen in the sequel that many of these features were later crowned by a western tower.

Buttresses of the developed form seen at Bradwell and Reculver appear also in the sixth-century churches of S. Vitale, Ravenna, S. Lorenzo Maggiore, Milan, and elsewhere in Italy; but they were mainly used as external abutments to an arch rather than as simple supports to a wall.

The consideration of the characteristics of the plan of the Kentish group of churches, though somewhat incon-

[1] *Forschungen in Salona*, 1917.
[2] A. Naef, 'Les dates de construction de l'église de Romainmôtier', in *Bull. Mon.*, lxx (1906), p. 425.

PLATE 4

MOSAIC FROM THE CHURCH AT TABARKA, TUNIS

PLATE 5

BRIXWORTH, NORTHANTS., INTERIOR LOOKING E.

c. 670

clusive, may be said generally to point to an Italian origin, with a strong Eastern rather than Roman influence, which, however, may well have been supplied from within the Greek exarchate or even Rome itself, and not necessarily from farther afield.

Before turning to the Northumbrian group of early churches, which present a very marked difference from the Kentish type, it would be well to consider the architectural results of the immediately succeeding period in the southern half of the island. This period is marked by a more ambitious type of building, which reflects not only the greater security of the church but the marked intellectual and ecclesiastical revival which was the result of the arrival of Archbishop Theodore and Abbot Adrian. The monuments of the latter part of the seventh century are comparatively few in number; but amongst them is one of prime importance, the church at Brixworth (Northants), while Heane's church at Abingdon, known only from literary sources, is nevertheless a landmark not only in English but in European architectural history. Few, if any, other churches can be definitely dated to this period, but of these the nave of St. Martin's, Canterbury, is a probable candidate.

The church at Brixworth[1] (Fig. 11) is perhaps the most imposing architectural memorial of the seventh century yet surviving north of the Alps. It is an aisled basilica of four bays (Pl. 5) with a triple arcade, now destroyed, at the east end, opening into a square presbytery with an apse beyond. The aisles have been removed, as has also a range of annexes at the west end, with the exception of a central porch which supports a later tower. There is every reason to associate this building with the church erected by the monks of Peterborough about 670.[2] The triple arcaded

---

[1] *Arch. Journ.*, lxix (1912), p. 505. Description by Professor Hamilton Thompson. For the early excavations see C. F. Watkins, *The Basilica and Basilican Church of Brixworth*, 1867.

[2] Sparke, *Hist. Ang. Scrip.* (Hugo Candidus), p. 9.

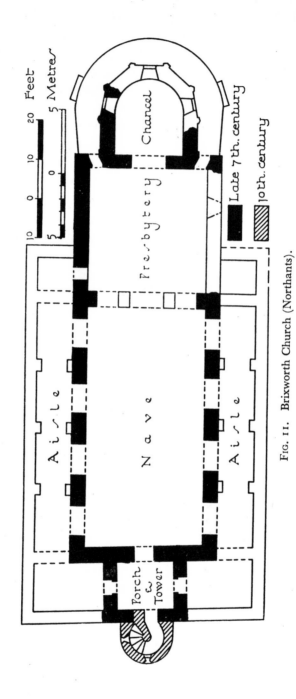

Feet

Metres

Chancel

Presbytery

Aisle

Nave

Aisle

Porch & Tower

Late 7th. century

10th. century

FIG. 11. Brixworth Church (Northants).

chancel-arch, the form of the apse,[1] and the annexes at the west end all equate so definitely with the corresponding features of the Kentish group as to leave no doubt as to the close relationship of Brixworth with that group both in date and character. The church is built of rubble with the arches turned in two rings of Roman bricks; the workmanship of these arches displays the sloping springers (Pl. 6) used in Roman work, but is otherwise so much more defective than Italian work of a like nature as to imply that Brixworth is the work of Saxon masons. The general effect of the building, however, is one of great spaciousness and strength, which would be greatly enhanced if the main arcades were not blocked and the aisles destroyed. A number of features of this church deserve special consideration. The apse is of the same form as that at Reculver, except that it has projecting pilasters at the angles, from which spring shallow wall-arches on the face of each bay. It seems evident that the apse was designed to enclose a crypt, of which there are now no remains except the encircling corridor, built outside the main wall, which will be further considered on a subsequent page. The square presbytery has at the west end of the north wall an original doorway, but any trace of the corresponding doorway in the south wall, if it existed, has been destroyed by a later arcade; it is not improbable that this doorway indicates an arrangement of sacristies similar to that at Bradwell, and of which the southern chamber was approached from the south aisle. The west porch, which now forms the base of the tower, is of the same form as that at Reculver, and has original arches on the north, south, and west faces. The north and south arches opened into adjoining chambers or porticus, of two stories, which are evidenced by the broken-off junctions of their now destroyed walls. That the porch had an upper story is indicated

[1] Professor Hamilton Thompson considers that there is structural evidence of the later rebuilding of the upper part of the apse, but if so it would appear probable that the early form was retained.

by the still partly surviving opening into the nave. The clearstory of the nave is pierced by large windows, with arched heads turned, like the main arches, in Roman brick.

The church at Abingdon, built by Heane about 680, is described in the Abingdon Chronicle [1] as being 120 ft. long and round both at the east and west ends. It stood across the southern part of the site of the medieval cloister; but the excavations of a few years ago failed to bring to light any trace of its structure. The dimension shows that it was a building of considerable scale, which can hardly have been without aisles, but its chief importance lies in the mention of the double apse at a date a century before the earliest example in Germany. Indeed, the only definite example of earlier date appears to be the basilica of Orléansville [2] (Algeria) built in 324, to which a western apse was added in 473 to serve as a burial-chapel for Bishop Reparatus, and was consequently no part of the original design. It is obvious that so unusual a feature can hardly have originated in England; and were no earlier examples available it would throw the gravest doubts on the veracity of the record. It has been shown that such structural examples have not yet come to light, but the researches of Princeton University in Syria [3] have revealed in certain Syrian churches a curious feature which may throw some light on the problem. In the central part of that country there exist four churches (Fig. 12), all of the normal basilican plan and dating from the fifth or sixth century, which are provided in the middle of the nave with a ritual enclosure in the form of a western apse enclosed by a low curved wall and screens. It should be remembered that few

---

[1] *Chronicon Monasterii de Abingdon* (Rolls Ser.), ii, p. 272: 'erat rotundum, tam in parte occidentali quam in parte orientali.'

[2] S. Gsell, *Les Monuments Antiques de l'Algérie*, ii, p. 238.

[3] Princeton Expedition to Syria, ii, *Ancient Architecture*, Sec. B. Plans of the churches at Il Firdjeh, Mirayeh, Kalota, and Kharab Shems, all showing the western choir, are reproduced.

of the Syrian churches have been excavated, and that the
preservation of four of these ritual enclosures above the
surface argues the existence of a far larger number, now
concealed by soil and debris. The authors of the report of
the Expedition do not commit themselves to any definite
theory as to the purpose of these structures, but suggest
that they may have served, in some sort, as the choir of the

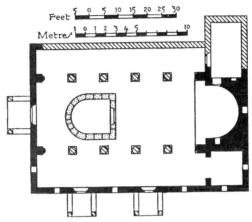

FIG. 12.   Kalota, Syria.

women who occupied the western part of the church.
However this may be, it requires only the translation
of a ritual arrangement into a structural one to produce
the double-apse plan. Eastern influence was strong in the
English church in 680, and one is tempted to hazard the
suggestion that the church of Abingdon may have been
designed to accommodate one of those double monasteries
of monks and nuns so common in England at that time,
and of which there are traces at Abingdon itself. It must,
however, be noted that in the double monastery of Kildare [1]
in Ireland the timber church had a partition running longi-
tudinally down the nave and dividing the women on the
north from the men on the south; thus indicating that in
Ireland, at least, it was the early custom to divide the sexes

[1] Cogitosus, *Vita Brigittae* (Migne, *Patr. Lat.* lxxii, 789), and Colgan, *Trias
Thaumaturga* (1647).

by a longitudinal partition and not by a transverse one as
in Syria and Egypt.

The nave of St. Martin's church, Canterbury[1] (Fig. 7),
is a structure of mixed rubble and Roman brick with
buttresses of the Bradwell type and remains of a very high
arch in the western wall. This arch rises 17 or 18 ft. above
the floor, but the lower part is disguised by the medieval
west doorway. It seems probable that the original arrangement was the same as at Brixworth, namely, two arches, one
above the other, opening into the two stories of a western
porch now replaced by the medieval tower. The arch is
flanked by two original windows of fair size and with heads
turned partly in Roman bricks.

The Northumbrian Group

The Northumbrian group of early churches presents, as
has been said, a marked difference from the rather earlier
group in the south, but the number of individual examples
is small and the evidence of date is not so conclusive.
Professor Baldwin Brown[2] accepts, as belonging to this
group, portions of the churches at Monkwearmouth and
Jarrow, the church at Escomb, and a portion of the church
at Corbridge. Of these the literary evidence of the founding
of the first two is exact, but the other two must be judged
by their style only. Monkwearmouth[3] is the most important of the group, as there seems no valid reason to doubt
its identity with the building of Benedict Biscop (c. 675). The
surviving portions indicate a nave 65 ft. by 19 ft. with a
two-storied porch (Pl. 7) at the west end and 'porticus'
opening to the north and south of it; there is no evidence
of the form or size of the chancel. The walls are of rubble
with larger roughly squared stones at the angles. The nave
was of unusual height, 31 ft. to the base of the west gable.
The porch is the most interesting feature. It has a barrel-

[1] C. F. Routledge, *St. Martin's, Canterbury* (1898).
[2] Baldwin Brown, *op. cit.* (Architecture), 2nd edit., chap. v.
[3] C. C. Hodges, *The Reliquary* (1893), p. 141.

PLATE 6

BRIXWORTH, NORTHANTS., W. ARCH OF
S. ARCADE
c. 670

MONKWEARMOUTH, DURHAM, DETAIL OF
W. PORCH
c. 675

PLATE 7

MONKWEARMOUTH, DURHAM, W. FRONT BEFORE
RESTORATION

c. 675, *with added* 10th-century tower

vault of stone, and the round-headed outer archway has responds (Pl. 6) of a very remarkable nature. The tall plinth is composed of two stones the width of the opening and carved with a pair of intertwined animals with long beaks; on the plinth stands a pair of turned stone balusters supporting a heavy impost; the whole effect is extremely barbaric. In the head of the gable of the porch was a large standing figure in relief, now almost entirely weathered away, and above the doorway was a carved frieze. A doorway communicates with the nave at the level of the upper story of the porch and there are two round-headed windows flanking the porch at a higher level.

The only building of early date which now survives at Jarrow [1] is the existing chancel; this is a building of squared and coursed rubble (Pl. 8), $41\frac{1}{2}$ ft. by $15\frac{3}{4}$ ft., which was originally a nave and had a chancel of narrower width projecting to the east of it. In the south wall are three round-headed windows, of no great size, but reduced in opening at a later date. On the north side is an original round-headed doorway. The modern nave replaces an aisled building probably of pre-Conquest date, and in it is preserved a dedicatory inscription of 685. That this date applies to the existing chancel is by no means certain; and if it does, what was the date of the nave? The two together can obviously not have formed an initial design, and as they were only separated by the width of the early Norman tower they can hardly have been distinct buildings. It is perhaps best to admit that the early date of Jarrow chancel is not proven.

The church at Escomb (Fig. 13 and Pl. 9),[2] Durham, is built of squared and coursed rubble and consists of a chancel about 10 ft square and a nave $43\frac{1}{2}$ ft. by $14\frac{1}{2}$ ft. The windows are either square or round-headed with internal splays, and the doorways have square heads and the jambs

---

[1] *Ibid.*, p. 148.
[2] Baldwin Brown, *op. cit.* (Architecture), 2nd edit., p. 136.

are rebated like the doorways at Monkwearmouth. The chancel-arch is tall, narrow, and round-headed; the voussoirs are set in true radial manner, and there are plain chamfered imposts at the springing-level. Professor Baldwin Brown considers that this is actually a re-erected Roman arch.

The church at Corbridge[1] has similar details with a considerable quantity of re-used Roman material, including the arch between the nave and the west porch. The outer

FIG. 13.   Escomb Church, Durham.   (Scale 16 ft. to 1 in.)

doorway of the porch has rebated jambs and the porch itself was subsequently carried up as a tower. The nave at Corbridge was 48 ft. by 17½ ft. and about 29 ft. high to the roof-plate. A distinguishing feature of both Escomb and Corbridge is that the arch and jamb-stones are carried completely through the wall, forming a lining to the openings. This is a feature probably copied from Roman work in the neighbouring sites of Corstopitum and Binchester, stations on or near the Wall.

It should be borne in mind that the dating of this Northumbrian group of churches is by no means as certain as that of the Kentish group, and depends on the equation of the existing work at Monkwearmouth and Jarrow with that of Benedict Biscop; and this cannot be taken as absolutely proven. Accepting, however, the probable hypothesis of the early date of the group, a few remarks may be made on the remarkable difference in type between it and the

[1] C. C. Hodges, *The Reliquary* (1893), p. 11.

PLATE 8

JARROW, DURHAM, S. WALL OF EARLY NAVE

c. 685

PLATE 9

a. S. side

b. N. wall of nave, late 7th or early 8th century

ESCOMB, DURHAM

southern group, for which the literary evidence perhaps provides some elucidation.

The Kentish churches were either the work of, or inspired by, the Italian mission of St. Augustine, reinforced at a later date by the Greco-Italian influence of St. Theodore. The Northumbrian group, including the churches of Monkwearmouth and Jarrow, are presumably the work of Benedict Biscop, who is recorded by Bede [1] to have brought masons from Gaul for this purpose. It has been shown that the Kentish churches present some marked affinities with certain Italian churches and none with those of Gaul; it must now be considered if it is otherwise with the Northumbrian group and if this group in any way illustrates the literary evidence. It should be premised, however, that the number of examples available for comparison is so meagre, on both sides, as to render any conclusions entirely tentative. The most distinctive features of the Northumbrian group are (a) an unusual length of nave, the proportions of length to breadth being as 3 to 1 or less; (b) a chancel of small proportions and of much less width than the nave; and (c) the considerable height of the side-walls of the building. Comparing these features with those of the Kentish group, it will be seen that the proportions of the naves of the latter group are on the average as $1\frac{1}{2}$ or $1\frac{3}{4}$ to 1; the apses are nearly and sometimes quite as wide as the nave, and the height of the walls is generally less noticeable, though here the evidence is largely lacking. Furthermore the triple arcaded chancel-arch is unknown in the north of England.

The available evidence in regard to contemporary French churches is singularly scanty, such structures as

[1] Bede, *Historia Abbatum*, chap. v. The Gaulish masons were to build a stone church after the manner of the Romans (*more Romanorum*). This expression was not uncommonly used in northern Gaul itself to designate the type of work then used south of the Loire. Another expression, 'manu gothica', with the same significance, is used in connexion with the abbey of S. Pierre, Rouen (later S. Ouen), in 535 (A. Masson, *L'église Saint Ouen de Rouen*, p. 7).

survive being almost entirely of a special character, such as
the Baptistery of St. John at Poitiers, the Hypogeum near the
same place, and the crypts of S. Laurent at Grenoble and
elsewhere. The foundations of one church of comparatively
small size have, however, been uncovered at S. Similien,
Nantes.[1] The west end was not discovered, but sufficient
of the body of the church was uncovered to indicate that its
proportions must have approached those of the Northumberland group, and its apse was a narrow structure projecting from the middle of the east wall. That length in
proportion to breadth was a feature of some of the churches
of Gaul is perhaps indicated by the plan of the fifth-century
church of S. Pierre at Vienne. Beyond this point it is
impossible to pursue the inquiry until more evidence is
supplied by excavation, but it may be noted that the earlier
part of St. Martin's church, Canterbury, approaches more
nearly to the Northumbrian model than the Kentish, which
may indicate that it was rebuilt by Bertha and her Gaulish
chaplain in their native manner before the advent of St.
Augustine. The proportions of the nave at Bradwell also
do not accord with those of the Kentish group (being rather
more than 2 to 1), and here, it may be, is to be found a
blend of the Northumbrian school represented by Bishop
Cedd and the southern method of building.

The general effect of the Northumbrian group of churches
is far more barbaric than that of the southern group, and
there is little doubt that in this it reflects the contemporary
work of Merovingian Gaul, which, as may be seen in the
Hypogeum at Poitiers, is almost equally barbaric, though
more richly ornamented, than the English examples. This
building [2] provides also a remarkable illustration of the

[1] *Soc. Arch. de Nantes*, xxxv, p. 176. The same uncertainty exists as to the proportions of the church of S. Christophe de Suèvres, which has been identified
with much probability with a church founded about 675. See *Congrès Arch.
de France* (Blois, 1925), p. 525.

[2] C. de la Croix, *Hypogée Martyrium de Poitiers* (1883). The author assigns the
building to near the beginning of the seventh century.

identity or close kinship of the two schools in the incised
figures of angels on stone slabs (Fig. 14) which formed part
of its ornament; they are so similar in drawing and execution to the figures on St. Cuthbert's coffin at Durham [1] that

FIG. 14. 1. Poitiers, Hypogeum, stone slab. 2. Durham, St. Cuthbert's
coffin, wood board.

there can be little doubt of their common origin. To the
north of England, however, came a far more able group
of sculptors who were responsible for the high crosses and
other works, and whose contemporaneity with the Merovingian craftsmen has caused not a little confusion in the
classification of Northumbrian art.

Before leaving the subject of the Northumbrian churches,
some consideration must be given to the four churches
which Wilfrid built or restored at Hexham, Ripon, and

[1] Haverfield and Greenwell, *Catalogue of Sculptured Stones in the Library at
Durham*, p. 133.

York. Of the churches at Hexham and Ripon there exist contemporary descriptions from the pen of Eddius, Wilfrid's biographer, and at both places there still exist crypts, of the type known as a *confessio*, which evidently formed parts of Wilfrid's structures. The information with regard to Hexham (Fig. 15) has recently been supplemented by certain discoveries made when the modern nave was built a few years ago.[1] It is, however, greatly to be regretted that this unique opportunity for ascertaining the precise plan and

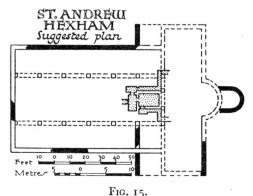

FIG. 15.

dimensions of Wilfrid's minster was largely thrown away, and the notes made at the time are unsatisfactory and inconclusive. The description of Eddius,[2] supplemented by that of Prior Richard of Hexham, indicates a church of considerable size with colonnades to the nave, aisles with galleries above, chapels, probably in the aisles, crypt, turret staircases, and other structures. The foundations and remains of walls on the spot permit the identification of the north and west walls of the nave and imply the existence of a transept. The foundation of an apse of comparatively narrow span (15 ft.) found under the existing choir may

[1] Baldwin Brown, *op. cit.* (Architecture), 2nd edit., chap. vi.
[2] Eddius, *Vita Wilfridi*, chap. xxii: 'domum . . . fundavit, cuius profunditatem in terra cum domibus mire lapidibus fundatam, et super terram multiplicem domum columnis variis et porticibus multis suffultam, mirabilique longitudine et altitudine murorum ornatam et variis liniarum anfractibus viarum, aliquando sursum aliquando deorsum per cochleas circumductam.'

either be part of St. Wilfrid's work or more probably an addition thereto. The chief difficulty in connexion with the plan is the position of the crypt, which, to accord with any probable hypothesis, must have been under the nave, whereas its normal position, according to most continental analogies, should be under the high altar. It must, however, be borne in mind that this position is not universal, even in Italy, the *confessio* under the church of St. Stephen on the Latin Way, Rome, being under the east end of the nave.[1] Furthermore the idea underlying the normal placing of the altar over the *confessio* was that it should mark to the public eye the precise place of burial of the saint or martyr in the crypt below. In the church of Wilfrid there could be no question of such intention, as the church stood on a virgin site with no earlier Christian traditions attaching to it. The apparent evidence of the remains may therefore be accepted—that here the crypt was designed to lie below the east end of the nave. The evidence of the position of the south wall of Wilfrid's church is inconclusive, but if the crypt was placed axially the width of the nave with its aisles must have been some 62 ft. The position of the two entrance passages to the crypt would seem also to provide some evidence of the lines of the two arcades, the one passage perhaps debouching within the line of the south arcade and the other without the line of the north arcade. It should be added, however, that the excavations afforded evidence that was held to disprove this. Wilfrid's work at Hexham is mainly built of squared stone, consisting very largely of re-used Roman material. The crypt has a plain barrel-vault, quite well constructed, but is entirely devoid of structural ornament. The restoration suggested in the accompanying plan will be found to bear a close general resemblance to that of the early church of St. Denis, generally attributed to Dagobert I (623–39).

With the exception of the very similar crypt at Ripon,

[1] See plan in Marucchi, *Éléments d'archéologie chrétienne* (2nd edit.), ii, p. 234.

no traces survive of any of the other three churches built by Wilfrid, and the only indication of their form and appearance is to be derived from literary sources. Of Ripon, Eddius [1] notes that it was built of smooth stone with numerous columns and porticus. At York Wilfrid restored the stone church completed by St. Oswald, but there are no recorded details of its form. Late in his life Wilfrid built a second church at Hexham; it was dedicated to St. Mary, and is described [2] as being in the form of a tower, almost round, and having porticus on the four sides. This is the earliest instance in this country of the centrally planned church, the consideration of which is reserved to a subsequent chapter.

The eighth century and the first half of the ninth is the most obscure and difficult period in the history of English architecture. Politically the headship of England had passed from Northumbria to Mercia, and the star of Wessex had not yet risen. That Mercia contained its full share of churches of cathedral or minster rank is well attested by the literary evidence, but though the district contains numerous remains of important stone sculpture of this age practically no structural remains of the greater churches have survived. The cathedrals of Lichfield, Leicester, Sidnacester, and Worcester have left no trace, and the same is true of the early buildings of the Abbeys of Ely, Peterborough, Bardney, Repton, the two Breedons, St. Albans, and the rest. Brixworth stands alone as an example of early Mercian architecture; and this, as we have seen, belongs to the seventh century. In other parts of England the paucity of examples is almost equally marked; throughout the country the first era of church-building and minster-founding was past, and the majority of churches built in the

[1] Eddius, *op. cit.*, chap. xvi: 'basilicam polito lapide a fundamentis in terra usque ad summum aedificatam variis columnis et porticibus suffultam in altum erexit et consummavit.'
[2] Richard of Hexham: 'in modum turris erecta et fere rotunda, a quatuor partibus totidem porticus habens' (Raine, *Hexham*, i, p. 14).

previous age probably survived intact until the Danish invasions. The building of the age was thus no doubt largely confined to the multiplication of the smaller rural churches, where documentary evidence is necessarily lacking, and internal evidence is unrecognized and perhaps unrecognizable.

That the age was certainly not one of artistic apathy is indicated by the examples of stone carving surviving at Breedon (Leicestershire), Peterborough, Castor, Fletton, and in various parts of Derbyshire and Nottinghamshire, much of which must be assigned to this period, and the literary accounts of a few churches built or rebuilt in the eighth century give no indication of a decline from the standard of the previous age. In Northumbria, however, the steady degeneration in the stone sculpture reflects the feeble condition of the kingdom and the decay of social institutions due to political anarchy.

The literary evidence, alluded to above, concerns the churches of York, Glastonbury, and St. Albans. The church at York (it is uncertain if it was the cathedral or not) was built by Archbishop Albert 766–82; it is described by Flaccus Alcuinus[1] as being of appropriate height supported by columns and arches and surrounded by porticus; it had a great number of upper apartments with separate roofs and thirty altars. Two disciples, Eanbald and Alcuin, are said to have erected the building. It is evident from this description that the church not only possessed aisles but galleries or chambers above them as at Hexham.

A church is said to have been built[2] at Lichfield by Bishop Hedda (691–721), but nothing is known of its form or character.

Of the church erected by Ine of Wessex (689–728) at Glastonbury[3] it is recorded that it was larger than the

[1] *Historians of the Church of York* (Rolls Ser.), no. 71, 1. lxi.
[2] Thomas of Chesterfield, Wharton's *Anglia Sacra*, i, p. 428
[3] See Armitage Robinson, 'The Historical Evidence as to the Saxon Church at Glastonbury', in *Proc. Somerset Arch. and N. H. Soc.*, lxxiii (1927), p. 40.

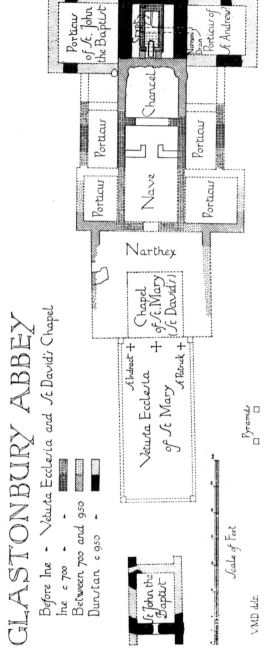

GLASTONBURY ABBEY

Before Ine = Vetusta Ecclesia and St David's Chapel
Ine c. 700 = "
Between 700 and 950 = "
Dunstan c. 950 = "

Porticus
of St. John
the Baptist

Crypt

Norman
Drain

Porticus of
St Andrew?

Chancel

Porticus

Porticus

Porticus

Nave

Porticus

Porticus

Narthex

Chapel
of St. Mary
(St. David's)

Abbract +

Vetusta Ecclesia
of St Mary

+
St Mary

St Patrick +

Pyramids

St John the
Baptist

Scale of Feet

VMD delt.

Fig. 16.

earlier *vetusta ecclesia* and immediately to the east of it. It survived in part, with later additions on the east and the earlier timber church on the west, till the Norman Conquest, the two churches being distinguished as the *major ecclesia* and the *vetusta ecclesia* respectively. The size of the wooden church was said to have been exactly reproduced in the existing Lady Chapel, 60 ft. by 26 ft., which gives some idea of the scale of Ine's greater church. Quite recently (1927–8) the remains of a pink *opus signinum* floor and foundations have been uncovered under the later nave at Glastonbury, which are, with little doubt, part of Ine's building. They show the east end of a nave with flanking porticus and a wide chancel-arch. The chancel of this church was rebuilt on a square plan at some subsequent date and at the same period aisles or porticus were added at the west end of Ine's nave and also enclosing a building which has been identified with the chapel or chancel added by St. David (sixth century) to the *vetusta ecclesia*[1] (Fig. 16).

Of Offa's church at St. Albans our information is confined to William of Malmesbury's statement that it was a building of the most beautiful workmanship.[2]

Two village churches may be assigned to this period on the strength of carved work that they still retain *in situ* in their structures. The first of these is at Kirkby Hill[3] in Yorkshire, where one impost of the south doorway is carved with fairly early vine-scroll and good interlacing. The structure, of which it forms a part, is a small building 24¼ ft. by 15 ft., retaining no other early feature of interest; the chancel has been rebuilt. The second church at Britford,[4] Wilts., is a much more important building, retaining the whole of the nave (44 ft. 4 in. by 20 ft. 2 in.) with two remarkable arches at the east end opening into chambers,

---

[1] *Antiq. Journ.*, x, p. 24.
[2] 'Basilica pulcherrimi operis', *Gesta Pontif.* (Rolls Ser.), p. 316.
[3] Plan of building in *V.C.H., Yorks. N. Riding*, i, p. 370. Drawing of impost in *Yorks. Arch. Journ.*, xix, p. 338. Baldwin Brown dates the building ninth cent.
[4] Baldwin Brown, *op. cit.* (Architecture), p. 220.

now destroyed, to the north and south of the building.[1]
The vine-scroll decorations on the skeleton stone-framing
of the north archway (Pl. 10) would indicate by the stage of
its development a date of about 800. There are, on the
other hand, features of a later age, the most noticeable of
which is the presence of pilaster-strips and label in the side-
arches. If this feature be borrowed from Carolingian
models, as is maintained by Baldwin Brown, there is still
nothing against the suggested date, but the consideration
of this feature must be reserved to a later chapter.

Another possible example of this period is the church at
Hackness (Yorks.),[2] where the wide semicircular chancel-
arch has a sculptured impost on the north side. The nunnery
at Hackness was founded by St. Hilda and survived until
the Danish invasions. The impost bears an interlaced design
with the heads of birds which has certain affinities with the
carvings of the door-jambs at Monkwearmouth, but it is
very difficult to prove whether or no the impost is *in situ*.

The ruined chapel at Heysham (Lancs.),[3] a plain rectangular building (27 ft. by 8½ ft. average), exhibits the long
proportions of the early Northumbrian churches and the
internal rebate of the Reculver doorways. It has certain
Irish features, however, and has no chancel. The doorway
has a round head with grooved ornament and the jambs
have stone linings alternately set horizontally and vertically
as at Escomb. There is little to date this example, but the
survival of early features may indicate an eighth- or ninth-
century date.

The doorway at Heysham Chapel is paralleled at Somer-
ford Keynes (Wilts.) and, in its construction, at Heysham
parish church; and to these Baldwin Brown adds for various

---

[1] There is some slight evidence that part of the west wall of the north transept
at Britford is of the same date as the nave; if so, the two arches must have
opened into annexes in the angles of the transept analogous to the two flanking
towers at North Elmham to be described later.

[2] *V.C.H., Yorks. N. Riding*, ii, p. 530.

[3] Baldwin Brown. *op. cit.* (Architecture), 2nd edit., p. 187.

PLATE 10

BRITFORD, WILTS., ARCH IN N. WALL
OF NAVE

c. 800

PLATE 11

W. face   S. face

BEWCASTLE, CUMBERLAND, CROSS-SHAFT

c. 670

reasons parts of Sockburn-on-Tees, Bardsey (Yorks.), and possibly Titchfield (Hants) and Bishopstone (Sussex), placing them all provisionally in the eighth or ninth century.[1]

Before passing on to the consideration of the ornament of the pre-Danish period a few words must be said as to the general arrangement and subsidiary buildings of the early monasteries, a subject which has been illustrated by recent discoveries.

Benedictine monasticism, in spite of the influence of St. Augustine and St. Wilfrid, had but a short life and a narrow influence in seventh-century England. All that is known and all that has been recently discovered go to prove that the English monasteries of that age partook far more of the character of those of the Eastern and Celtic churches. The chief external features of this form of monastic institution consisted in the multiplication of small churches, in the provision of a separate cell for each monk, and in the surrounding of the whole by a bank, wall, or other enclosure. This enclosure was perhaps originally defensive, and the sites of many early monasteries, both in Ireland and England, were probably determined by the pre-existence of a defensive work of suitable character. Thus the Irish often made use of the circular cashels [2] erected by the Cruithni or others of a previous age; and in England seventh-century monasteries were set within the Roman defences of Burgh Castle and Reculver, and perhaps also at Othona and Dover. Where no such early enclosures existed, they were, however, supplied by the newcomers, and thus Iona Abbey [3] was surrounded by a bank, Abingdon [4] by a wall, and Oundle [5] by a thick hedge of thorns. The multiplication of churches within the enclosure cannot be

[1] Baldwin Brown, *op. cit.* (Architecture), 2nd edit., chap. vii.
[2] H. C. Lawlor, *The Monastery of St. Mochaoi of Nendrum* (1925).
[3] Adamnan, *Life of St. Columba*, Bk. II, xxix.
[4] *Chronicon Monasterii de Abingdon* (Rolls Ser.), ii, p. 272.
[5] Eddius, *Vita Wilfridi* (ed. Colgrave), chap. lxvii, pp. 146–7.

considered as entirely a Celtic practice, for something similar is found even in Rome, where St. Gregory's own abbey on the Caelian Hill had several dependent churches and oratories, and St. Peter's was likewise the centre of a group of churches; but whereas in Rome these structures are obviously subsidiary to the main church, in the Celtic groups the various churches are much of a size. The remains at Clonmacnois and Glendalough are familiar examples of the practice, which was probably equally common in England. Thus St. Augustine's abbey at Canterbury had three churches, nearly contemporary. Monkwearmouth and Malmesbury had also three; the survival of early dedications would seem to imply the same thing in London. Glastonbury had a series of churches and St. Wilfrid built two or more at Hexham.[1] A further peculiarity is noticeable at Canterbury, where the three early churches are placed roughly on the same axial east and west line. This may perhaps be a conscious imitation of the arrangement then existing at St. Peter's at Rome, or it may have its root in some unconscious tradition of pagan alignments. In any case it can hardly be accidental, and may well have been reproduced again in London with the cathedral of St. Paul and the churches of St. Gregory and St. Augustine, and at Glastonbury.[2]

The domestic portion of the early monasteries consisted, as has been said, of separate cells for the monks, with a common refectory, a guest-house, and other buildings. These arrangements have recently been illustrated, in a highly remarkable manner, by the discovery of the remains of St. Hilda's Abbey at Whitby. The excavations here have uncovered a considerable number of separate cells, all

[1] According to Richard of Hexham, Wilfrid built churches of St. Peter and St. Michael at Hexham, besides those of St. Andrew and St. Mary. See Raine's *Priory of Hexham* (Surtees Soc.), i, p. 18.

[2] At Fontenelle (S. Wandrille) there was a chapel of St. Pancras very closely analogous in position to that at St. Augustine, Canterbury, and perhaps indicating a similar early arrangement.

of rectangular form and built of the roughest masonry. There is, on the other hand, evidence of considerable care for drainage and provision of ovens and cooking-places. One larger building has also been uncovered, which may be provisionally identified with the refectory; but the church or churches of the monastery still lie concealed or destroyed under the twelfth- and thirteenth-century abbey church. Separating the cells are areas of rough stone paving, and there are traces of several stone-paved roadways leading from one part of the monastery to another. Running through the uncovered part of the site was apparently a ditch into which the individual drains from the cells discharged themselves. A much smaller portion of a very similar type of establishment was excavated in 1912 at Llantwit Major near Cardiff.[1] This abbey, the centre of influence of St. Illtyd, was one of the largest and most celebrated monastic establishments in Wales. It supplied not a few of the evangelists of Brittany and flourished until its destruction by the Northmen late in the tenth century. The excavations here disclosed a group of stone-built cells, very similar in form and character to those at Whitby, but better constructed though not necessarily of a later date, as here the remote tradition of Roman building had suffered no violent break. An interesting literary source gives evidence of yet a third establishment of a like nature. The abbey of Abingdon, founded by Heane about 675, is described in the Abingdon Chronicle [2] as consisting, besides the church, which has already been dealt with, of twelve cells (*habitacula*), each with an oratory, without a cloister, but surrounded by a wall which did duty as a cloister. This last expression, if we take it in its medieval

---

[1] *Arch. Camb.*, 6th ser., xv, p. 141.

[2] *Chronicon Monasterii de Abingdon* (Rolls Ser.), ii, p. 272: 'In circuitu hujus monasterii erant habitacula xii et totidem capellae et in habitaculis xii monachi ibidem manducantes et bibentes et dormientes; nec habebant clausum (? claustrum) sicut nunc habent sed erant circumdati muro alto qui erat eis pro claustro.'

sense and not simply as an enclosure, finds a remarkable illustration in the excavations made in 1924 on the site of the abbey of St. Mochaoi at Nendrum[1] (Co. Down). Here it was found that a well-paved walk extended for a considerable distance along the inside of the inner enclosing wall of the monastery, and no doubt served some of the purposes of the later monastic cloister.

Finally, at St. Augustine's, Canterbury, a small rectangular building has been recently discovered under, and lying diagonally across, the medieval Frater. It may well have been one of the buildings of the early monastery, the remainder of which lay under or near the medieval cloister-garth.

[1] H. C. Lawlor, *The Monastery of Saint Mochaoi of Nendrum* (1925).

Chapter III

PERIOD OF THE HEPTARCHY

Ornament and Fittings

A NUMBER of fortuitous circumstances have rendered the study of early English Ornament an exceedingly difficult subject, and has made it the arena of a prolonged controversy which is even now not finally decided. Two main causes have contributed to this unfortunate situation: firstly, the almost complete absence of surviving ornament in definitely dated structures of the early period; and, secondly, the circumstance that the great mass of ornament which does survive is exemplified in isolated monuments, chiefly standing-crosses, which can only be exactly dated by historical inscriptions. Such inscriptions certainly exist; but in no instance have they come down to us sufficiently intact to render their interpretation and application beyond dispute. Thus we have twelfth-century evidence that high crosses stood at the head and foot of the grave of Acca, Bishop of Hexham (d. 740), one of which (Pl. 14) bore his epitaph; both these crosses have in all probability survived in a fragmentary state, but the essential part of the inscription is missing. Again, the Bewcastle cross (Pl. 11) has a Runic inscription, read by many, and amongst them the latest, authorities as referring to Alchfrith, son of Oswy of Northumbria; but the characters are too weathered to render the interpretation certain, and other authorities refuse to accept it as evidence.

The result is that the subject must be approached on stylistic and kindred grounds, with a proper regard to the historical and geographical background of each individual example. Inquiry, even on these lines, does not, however, evade controversy, for apart from the inevitable conflict of individual judgement there is the disputed value of analogical evidence drawn from other branches of the decorative arts. Thus it has been held that no sound argument can be based on an analogy between manuscript designs and stone-carving or between either of these and metal-work. Within certain limits, however, we hold that this type of evidence is allowable, for while it is obvious that the level of execution may be totally different in two branches of art, a peculiar decorative motif is unlikely to occur in one branch when it had been long abandoned in another. Thus the crude figure-drawing on St. Cuthbert's coffin (Fig. 14) or the Franks Casket is only evidence of the lack of skill of the wood- and bone-carvers, and is no evidence that the two works were not contemporary in date with a far higher level of achievement in stone-carving and manuscript. Indeed, there is excellent evidence that St. Cuthbert's coffin is, in fact, nearly contemporary with the Lindisfarne Gospels and the product of the same monastery; but the figure-drawing of the Gospels is infinitely better than that of the coffin. It is possible indeed that wood- and bone-carving was but little employed at the time, and that craftsmen had little or no opportunity to perfect themselves in these arts. Be this as it may, in the branches of stone-carving, manuscript, and metal-work a very high standard of execution was reached; and while each has its peculiar conventions, which hardly intrude on its neighbour's domain, a certain number of decorative motives are common to all three, and reach in all three an almost equal level of attainment.

The controversy on the date of the Anglian stone crosses has generally been focused on the two outstanding examples of their class, the crosses of Bewcastle and Ruthwell (Pls. 11, 12), the date assigned varying from the seventh to the twelfth centuries. The discussion, however, may now be said to have narrowed down the issue to two alternative dates, the latter part of the seventh century and the middle of the eighth. The earlier age is maintained by Professors

PLATE 12

W. face   S. face

RUTHWELL, DUMFRIES, CROSS-SHAFT
late 7th century

Brøndsted and Baldwin Brown and the later by Mr. W. G. Collingwood. The opinion of Professor Brøndsted [1] is based upon the comparative study of the vine and animal decorations of the whole series of Anglian crosses; the result forms a logical sequence which is so satisfactory, both stylistically and historically, that it may fairly claim to hold the field and transfer the onus of proof to the holders of any competitive theory. The conclusions of Professor Baldwin Brown [2] are in entire agreement with those of Brøndsted so far as the Bewcastle and Ruthwell crosses are concerned.

The alternative date proposed by Mr. Collingwood [3] is based upon the supposed date of the Acca cross (*c.* 740), which he looks upon as the initial example. The chief objection to his theory is the crowding of the whole series of pre-Danish crosses into a period of 130 years; it compels its author to place two works of vastly different artistic achievement within ten years of one another and to confine the rise, meridian, and decline of North Anglian Sculpture within a period of progressive political decadence.

The subject is one well worthy of the most careful study, for it deals with a series of stone monuments which (whichever theory prevails) is unparalleled and largely unrepresented elsewhere in Europe in the same age. Italian stone-sculpture of the seventh and eighth centuries is immeasurably inferior, while in France, at the same time, it practically did not exist. Ireland likewise produced, or at any rate has bequeathed, nothing of a like age; and the Celtic parts of Great Britain lagged still farther behind. We are confronted, therefore, with an art which, whatever its origins, stood largely alone, but was amazingly prolific, and attained levels which are seldom contemptible and sometimes remarkably high. Apart from the intrinsic value and interest of the sculptures themselves they sometimes, as we

---

[1] J. Brøndsted, *Early English Ornament*, English translation (1924).
[2] G. Baldwin Brown, *The Ruthwell and Bewcastle Crosses* (1921).
[3] W. G. Collingwood, *Northumbrian Crosses of the Pre-Norman Age* (1927).

have seen, form the only criteria for dating the architectural setting in which they occur.

In the following sketch of the development of this art the
sequence set forth by Professor Brøndsted will be adopted
and some additional reasons brought forward to support
its validity, but before considering the actual monuments
it will be well to review, shortly, the conditions which, we
hold, gave them birth. This aspect of the subject has been
treated most successfully by the late Bishop Forrest Browne,
who in a series of scattered publications has anticipated by
nearly a generation many of the conclusions arrived at by
the most recent writers on the subject.

The Italian mission of St. Augustine, though it brought
with it skilled masons and bricklayers, seems to have
attempted little or nothing in the decorative arts. The
tombs of the early archbishops which have survived at St.
Augustine's Abbey, Canterbury (Laurence, 619; Mellitus,
624; and Justus, 627), are plain masses of rubble enclosing
wooden coffins, their decoration, if any, being confined
to painting which has now perished.[1] With the arrival of
Theodore and Adrian, however, in 669, a new era seems
to have begun in the history of English art. We know nothing
of the men who accompanied the two ecclesiastics, but
Theodore was a Greek of Tarsus and Adrian was a native
of the African province of the Eastern Empire, driven from
his home by the Moslem conquest. The influence of the
two on the intellectual life of England was deep and lasting,
and may serve as some indication of their probable artistic
influence also. Theodore founded the school at Canterbury, and his influence is directly traceable in those of
Jarrow and York; as a result Greek was long taught in the
Anglo-Saxon schools, and in Bede's time there were still
living scholars of Theodore and Adrian to whom Greek and
Latin were as familiar as their native tongue. The Peni-
tential of Theodore is interesting in the same connexion.

[1] *Archaeologia*, lxvi, p. 388.

Time after time in it he gives the parallel usages of the Greek and Latin Churches on various points; and it is evident that the two systems must have been equally familiar to his scholars. That this influence of Theodore and Adrian was coextensive with the Heptarchy is evident from the perambulations which they undertook throughout the country, and is illustrated by the curious survival of two Neapolitan feasts in the calendar of Lindisfarne, due with little doubt to Adrian, who had been Abbot of Niridanum in the near neighbourhood of Naples. The schools of Theodore also acted as a strong counter-attraction to those of Ireland, which had hitherto held undisputed pre-eminence, for while large numbers of Englishmen still went to study in Ireland a certain number of Irish began to attend the English schools. It would appear to be precisely at the point when the Celtic or Irish Church in England lost the battle with the orthodox party, at the Synod of Whitby, 664, and retired from the contest, that the decorative arts began to make their appearance; and one is tempted to conclude that the Irish monks brought with them little but piety and learning, and it required the Greco-Italian leaven to galvanize the latent artistic talents of the Anglo-Saxons into activity. Certainly there is nothing in the surviving description of the early Irish monasteries at Iona and Lindisfarne to show that any attempt was made to decorate the timber and rude stone structures of which they were composed.

The literary evidences of foreign influence in English art of the next few generations are many and varied; and, apart from the frequent visits of many of the English kings and ecclesiastics to Italy and Gaul, we have three definite records of the introduction of foreign art or artists into this country. Benedict Biscop, who at the age of 25 visited Rome, accompanied Theodore to England and acted as head of the Canterbury school for two years. As Abbot of Monkwearmouth and Jarrow he built there in 675 and

681 the two churches which perhaps still partly survive. In connexion with the former, Bede records that he went over to Gaul and brought back with him masons to build a stone church after the Roman manner (*more Romanorum*). As this expression is also used, at the same period, in northern Gaul, it is evident that the Roman manner of building survived only in the southern part of the country, and Benedict's stay at Arles suggests that he brought his masons from Provence. Benedict paid in all five visits to Rome, bringing back with him books, paintings, and relics; paintings of both the Old and New Testaments decorated his two churches.[1]

St. Wilfrid, on his departure from Rome in 680 and 704, is recorded by Eddius to have collected relics and precious things 'too numerous to mention', and hangings of purple and silk for the adornment of his churches. He brought back with him also masons and artisans of all kinds.[2]

St. Aldhelm, Bishop of Sherborne (705–10), also visited Rome and brought back with him a white marble altar (4 ft. by 2¼ ft. by 1½ ft.) with a projecting rim and wrought all round with crosses.[3] He also possessed a chasuble, ornamented with black scrolls containing peacocks, evidently of foreign and probably of Eastern workmanship.[4] Aldhelm was a church-builder and erected churches at Malmesbury, Bradford-on-Avon, Frome, Sherborne, and Wareham, of which, unfortunately, no recognizable traces now remain.

Enough has been said to show the close intellectual and artistic contact between the early English church and Italy, Gaul, and the East, and we must now turn to observe how far this contact is reflected in the surviving monuments. That Eastern influence was, at any rate, present is indicated by such scenes as St. Paul and St. Anthony in the Desert on the Ruthwell Cross and by the use of the Greek blessing in English eighth-century manuscripts and carvings. In this,

[1] Bede, *Historia Abbatum*, ed. Plummer i, p. 368.
[2] Eddius Stephanus, *Vita Wilfridi* (ed. Colgrave), chap. xiv, pp. 30–1.
[3] William of Malmesbury, *Gesta Pontificum* (Rolls Ser.), p. 373.
[4] *Ibid.*, p. 365.

England only reflects the position in contemporary Rome and Ravenna. The influence of Italy and the possible influence of Gaul in purely architectural matters have already been dealt with, but the crux of the whole situation remains to be considered. If our dating be right we find that towards the close of the seventh century, more especially in northern England, there appears, suddenly, a whole series of sculptured stone monuments, of which the form is practically confined to these islands, the decoration is of superior execution to that found elsewhere, and the figure-sculpture is considerably in advance of any contemporary European sculpture; and all this without any of the preparatory phases leading up to the final achievement—an art springing fully armed from the head of a people but recently emerged from a barbaric state. It is obvious that such a thesis demands careful consideration; and we must firstly consider what definite evidence there is for the existence of English stone-sculpture of this age.

The inscriptions of the Bewcastle cross [1] are generally considered to contain references to King Oswy (644–70), Alchfrith, and Cuniburga (wife of Alchfrith and daughter of Penda of Mercia), dating the cross to about the year 670. But, as we have seen, the interpretation, though generally, is not universally accepted. We have, however, collateral evidence of just such a memorial at the same period in the history of William of Malmesbury. He relates [2] that there were in his day (c. 1125), in the cemetery of Glastonbury, two stone pyramids, one 28 ft. high and of five stages, with sculptured figures and a series of names which cannot now be identified; the other, 26 ft. high, was of four stages and bore the names Kentwin, Hedda the bishop, Bregored, and Beoward. Kentwin was King of Wessex 676–85, Hedda was Bishop of Wessex 677–705, and the other two were abbots of Glastonbury in the second half of the seventh and

---

[1] Baldwin Brown, *The Ruthwell and Bewcastle Crosses*, 2nd edit., chap. ix.

[2] William of Malmesbury, *Gesta Regum Anglorum* (Rolls Ser.), i, p. 25.

the beginning of the eighth century. We have thus reasonably good evidence that stone shafts generally similar to that at Bewcastle were erected at Glastonbury round about the year 700, for William of Malmesbury, apart from being a veracious historian, had no motive for inventing an inscription which he himself did not profess to understand.

In addition to this the same author records [1] that after the funeral procession of St. Aldhelm from Doulting to Malmesbury a stone cross was put up each seven miles of the journey. There is, however, nothing to indicate whether they were sculptured or not.

Again, the cross at Reculver (Pl. 20) was set upon a base (in front of the chancel-arch) which, at any rate, is contemporary with or earlier than the building, as the pink *opus signinum* pavement is stopped against it on two sides. [2] It is reasonable to suppose that the cross itself, of which fragments survive, is in part, at least, the original shaft set on this base, and thus dates from about 670. The original columns of the chancel-screen of the same church are enriched at the base with a well-executed key-pattern, which shows that the masons of that age could cut with care and precision.

We are thus, by cumulative evidence, justified in saying that sculptured crosses of this type were actually erected in the latter part of the seventh century, and must now turn to the origin of the form. This is traced, by both Baldwin Brown and Collingwood, to the earlier tradition represented by the upright stones, marked with the chrism, at Whithorn. The practice of setting up crosses of stone or wood to mark the site of a notable event is amply attested

[1] William of Malmesbury, *Gesta Pontificum* (Rolls Ser.), pp. 383–4.
[2] In the life of St. Willibald (born *c.* 700) occurs the statement that 'it is the custom of the Saxon race that, on many of the estates of nobles and good men, they are wont to have, not a church, but the standard of the Holy Cross, dedicated to our Lord and reverenced with great honour, lifted up on high'. It is thus possible that the church of Reculver was built round a pre-existing cross, which would account for its unusual position.

PLATE 13

ABERLADY, E. LOTHIAN, CROSS-SHAFT

late 7th century (now at Carlowrie)

CROFT, YORKS., CROSS-SHAFT

late 7th century

PLATE 14

HEXHAM, NORTHUMBERLAND,
ACCA'S CROSS
early 8th century (now at Durham)

ABERCORN, MIDLOTHIAN
CROSS-SHAFT
late 7th century

by the Irish records, the life of St. Kentigern, and other authorities; and there is no difficulty in accepting the origin of the custom as Celtic, even when we find it practised in the south of England, for Irish missionaries had founded monasteries at Malmesbury, in Sussex, and no doubt elsewhere before the arrival of the Saxon ecclesiastics. Glastonbury, of course, was a Hiberno-British monastery. We may, therefore, assume that the erection of high crosses, perhaps generally of timber, was an accepted practice before the arrival of Theodore, and that his age is responsible only for their sculptured decoration.

Of the purely decorative motives employed on the Anglian crosses the most common is the vine-scroll, with or without birds and beasts climbing in the foliage. This form is the basis of Brøndsted's analysis of the development and sequence of the series. He postulates an original introduction of the form by foreign craftsmen from the East in the seventh century and judges the age of each individual example by the degree of its approach to a rendering of the plant as expressed by one familiar with its growth in a natural state. Thus he starts his series with the Otley [1] cross-shaft, the Easby cross-shaft, and the Hovingham frieze, and passes on to the Croft stone (Pl. 13) and the Bewcastle (Pl. 11) and Ruthwell crosses (Pl. 12). It should, however, be pointed out that the motif was in common use not only in the East but also in the West,[2] under the late Empire, and even made its appearance in grave-furniture of the late pagan Saxon period in Sussex.[3] This, however, does not vitiate his argument, as there is a wide hiatus in the reproduction of the vine-scroll in stone, both in England and Gaul, and a single piece of no doubt imported metalwork can have no bearing on the renaissance of stone-carving in Northumbria. The striking parallel which he

[1] *Yorks. Arch. Journ.*, xxiii, p. 225.
[2] E.g. carved stonework in the museums of Sens, Dijon, and Saintes, on the arch at Besançon, &c.
[3] At Alfriston; see *Sussex Arch. Colls.*, lvii, Pl. xxix; now in the museum at Lewes.

and others have drawn between the design of the Otley shaft and that on the posts of the ivory throne at Ravenna is sufficient to suggest their common origin. The throne, however, probably dates from the fifth or early sixth century, and is thought to be Alexandrine work; it yet remains to be shown where such work was produced in the East a century or more later. The introduction of Eastern, or perhaps east Italian,[1] craftsmen is in any case the only reasonable explanation of the sudden appearance of such work in the north of England and the equally sudden appearance of figure-sculpture of no mean order. How far the surviving examples are the work of the foreign carver, and how far that of his native pupil, is extremely difficult to determine; but the presence of certain native features in the Ruthwell and Bewcastle crosses, combined with the awkwardness of some of the figures, seems to mark them as English work. On the other hand, the slab with scrolls and human figures at Hexham is almost certainly foreign work, and some have maintained that it is of Roman date, an opinion which derives no support from the surviving Roman stone-sculpture found in the stations on or near the Wall.

A few other cross-shafts in Northumbria may also be assigned to the seventh century, including those at Abercorn (Pl. 14), Aberlady (Pl. 13), Jedburgh, and the Spital cross at Hexham. The first two of these, which are of purely Anglian type, should, in all historical probability, date from the short episode of the Anglian See of Abercorn (681–5). It is not necessary to pursue in detail the gradual degeneration of the vine-motif through the eighth and ninth centuries in Northumbria, but some consideration must be given to the great shaft (Pl. 14) now at Durham which, in all probability, is that which stood at the head of Acca's

[1] This origin of the vine-scroll appears to me to be confirmed by the appearance both in Constantinople and Ravenna of the two forms of vine-plant (the true vine and ivy-vine) side by side, a conjunction which is found also in the earliest English examples.

PLATE 15

SANDBACH, CHESHIRE, CROSS-SHAFTS
late 8th century

PLATE 16

DACRE, CUMBERLAND, FRAGMENT
8th century

CROPTHORN, YORKS, CROSS-HEAD
8th century

grave at Hexham. Acca died in 740, and the design of the double vine-scroll on the cross, though conventionalized and somewhat rigid, is yet considerably nearer to the original plant than most of the earlier examples. This is so marked that Mr. Collingwood makes it the starting-point of his sequence with the consequent crowding of his later series, which we have already touched upon. The difficulty is avoidable in two ways, either by supposing that the meridian level of Northumbrian carving was maintained over a generation or two, or by assuming a fresh introduction of foreign artists. There is nothing improbable in this latter supposition, for Acca followed in the steps of Wilfrid and is known to have greatly enriched and decorated the church of Hexham. It may also be pointed out that the outbreak of the Iconoclastic movement in the Eastern Empire in 726 provides an eminently suitable historical background for the further introduction of Byzantine artists into the West.

In any case the difficulty is not insuperable, and the excellence of the Acca shaft is purely academic and implies no greater mastery than most of the examples of the earlier period already cited.

The birds and beasts which often accompany the vine-scroll are derived from the same Eastern original. The beast (Pls. 16, 19, 27), in Northumbrian art, generally acquired a slender graceful outline which is very characteristic, and it is to this type, in particular, that the term 'Anglian Beast' is applied.

The other chief decorative motives employed in stone-carving are the following:

(a) The Interlacement, which is almost universal and of infinite variety (Pls. 11, 25, 29). Its various forms have been analysed and described by Romilly Allen.[1] The interlace is equally prominent in seventh- and eighth-century English manuscripts and metal-work. It differs from the con-

---

[1] Romilly Allen, *Early Christian Monuments of Scotland*, Pt. II, p. 140.

temporary Italian interlace by being commonly of one or twofold strands, whereas the Italian form is commonly of threefold strands.

(*b*) The Fret (generally drawn diagonally) is of fairly common occurrence on the crosses and elsewhere, e.g. Abercorn,[1] Lindisfarne,[2] Northallerton,[3] Hurworth,[4] South Kyme,[5] and Breedon on the Hill (Pls. 25, 27).[6] It occupies a more prominent place in the manuscripts and forms the basis of a whole page of the Lindisfarne Gospels.

(*c*) The trumpet-spiral is of very uncommon occurrence in English stone-carving. It occurs, however, at South Kyme (Pl. 28) and Breedon, and in a degraded form, with the trumpet-ends omitted, at Bradford-on-Avon, Elmstone Hardwick (Glos.), and on the font at Deerhurst (Pl. 55). It forms, on the other hand, one of the staple motives of the English manuscripts of the same age, from which it entirely disappears after the middle or end of the ninth century.[7]

(*d*) The checker-pattern occurs on the Bewcastle cross and at Hoddom and Hexham. It is, however, uncommon both in stone-carving and manuscript. A variant forming a diaper of small crosses is represented on a slab at Bradford-on-Avon and on the Irton cross (Pl. 17).

(*e*) The pelta-ornament[8] does not appear before the latter part of the eighth century, when it occurs at Breedon

---

[1] Romilly Allen, *Early Christian Monuments of Scotland*, Pt. II, p. 418.

[2] *Archaeologia*, lxxiv, Pl. LIII, cross-shaft vi.

[3] *Yorks. Arch. Journ.*, xix, p. 373.

[4] Haverfield and Greenwell, *Cat. of Sculptured Stones in the Library at Durham*, p. 95.

[5] *Antiq. Journ.*, iii, p. 118.

[6] *Archaeologia*, lxxvii, p. 226.

[7] The appearance of the trumpet-spiral in its developed form on enamelled bronze bowl-scutcheons, assigned to the beginning of the seventh century and found in various parts of England, would seem to indicate the early adoption by the Anglo-Saxons of this Celtic motif (see *Archaeologia*, lvi, p. 39; *Proc. Soc. Ants.*, xxii, p. 66; and *Antiq. Journ.*, v, p. 168, for examples). The finding of only one example in Ireland, and this of doubtful provenance, indicates that it was not from this source that the motif was borrowed.

[8] The history of this ornament on the Continent is treated by P. Deschamps in *Bull. Mon.* (1921), p. 255, and (1925), p. 95. See also *Archaeologia*, lxxvii, p. 227.

(Pl. 26*a*) and Fletton and in the English Codex Aureus at Stockholm (Pl. 23).

The great preponderance in numbers of the seventh- and eighth-century crosses in Northumbria, as compared with other parts of England, reflects primarily the early political superiority of the northern kingdom, but the universal abundance of suitable stone was no doubt also a contributary cause.

Crosses of this age are much less common, though not rare, in the midland counties, but here none survives of earlier date than the eighth century, thus reflecting the comparatively late conversion of the Mercian kingdom and its still later accession to supreme power. The counties of Cheshire, Derbyshire, Nottinghamshire, and Staffordshire, however, retain a number of notable examples, such as Sandbach (Cheshire) (Pl. 15), Bradbourne [1] (Derbyshire) (Pl. 18), Bakewell [2] (Derbyshire), Stapleford [3] (Notts.), Eyam (Derbyshire) (Pl. 17), &c. A remarkable and isolated example is to be found at Newent [4] (Forest of Dean) (Pl. 19); it perhaps dates from early in the eighth century, and the carving includes figure subjects and an Anglian beast of pure Northumbrian type. In the south of England there is a very marked scarcity of these memorials, partly reflecting the corresponding scarcity of suitable stone and partly resulting from the subsequent economic history of the southern part of the island. It must be remembered that throughout the Middle Ages and down to comparatively modern times the north has been but sparsely inhabited, thus removing the prime cause for the destruction of these memorials, whereas in the midlands and the south a gradually growing and more progressive population has destroyed, or re-used for other purposes, the great majority of the works of a previous age which had lost their signifi-

[1] *Arch. Journ.*, xlv, and *Reliquary and Illustrated Archaeologist*, x.
[2] Brøndsted, *Early English Ornament*, p. 66.
[3] *Arch. Journ.*, lxxiii, p. 203.
[4] *Reliquary and Illustrated Archaeologist*, xiii (1907), p. 197.

cance. The occasional survivors in the south of England make up for their scarcity by their unusual interest, this being especially the case with the cross at Reculver (Kent). As the decoration of this cross consists chiefly of figure-sculpture it may serve as an introduction to a consideration of this form of decoration, which is one of the chief features of the pre-Danish crosses throughout the country, and is not dealt with in Professor Brøndsted's survey.

We have seen that there is good evidence for the existence of a cross with sculptured figures at Glastonbury about 700 and, if Mr. Peers is right in his conclusions, the cross at Reculver (Pl. 20) should be nearly contemporary. The Northumbrian series starts at about the same time, the date suggested by the Bewcastle inscription being about 670. There is, however, little in common between the Reculver sculptures and the early Northumbrian works. The former at present stands alone as an example, more especially of drapery, rendered with a restrained freedom which is almost Greek. The northern series, of which Bewcastle (Pl. 11), Ruthwell (Pl. 12), Easby, Hoddom, Rothbury (Pl. 18), and Bishop Auckland [1] are the most remarkable examples, falls considerably below the Reculver standard, but the figures are generally well balanced and dignified compositions which only betray the unpractised hand in certain minor features. The drapery, however, is generally crudely rendered in detail, while remaining true in its main lines. Whatever may be the origin of the two types, it is obvious that they belong to widely different schools, and we are once again confronted with the baffling fact that we are unacquainted with any contemporary stone-sculpture elsewhere of the same class as either the southern or northern English type. It is unlikely that sculpture of the northern type could have been produced by native

[1] For Ruthwell and Bewcastle see Baldwin Brown's monograph; for Easby, W. G. Collingwood in *Yorks. Arch. Journ.*, xix, pp. 312–14; for Hoddom, *Roy. Com. on Hist. Mons. (Scotland), Dumfriesshire*, p. 101; and Bishop Auckland, *V.C.H., Durham*, i, p. 218.

PLATE 17

IRTON, LANCS., CROSS
9th century

EYAM, DERBYSHIRE, CROSS
late 8th century

PLATE 18

BRADBOURNE, DERBYSHIRE, CROSS-SHAFT

late 8th century

ROTHBURY, NORTHUMBERLAND, THE ASCENSION

late 7th or early 8th century

PLATE 19

MASHAM, YORKS., CROSS-
SHAFT

early 8th century

NEWENT, GLOUCESTER-
SHIRE, CROSS-SHAFT

mid 8th century

PLATE 20

RECULVER, KENT, FRAGMENT OF CROSS-SHAFT
late 7th century

LINDISFARNE, NORTHUMBERLAND, 'PILLOW-
STONE' OF BEANNA
8th century

artists, at any rate without foreign instruction, and it is far more unlikely, not to say impossible, that they produced the work at Reculver. We have seen that the general condition of southern Europe at the time provides an ample excuse, and the mission of Theodore and Adrian a suitable channel, for the introduction of artists of almost any southern or eastern nation into England; and if it could only be shown that somewhere in Italy or the East such sculpture was being produced within a generation of the English work, the difficulty would disappear. Italy and Africa, however, have nothing of the sort to show; contemporary Coptic sculpture is immeasurably inferior; and Syria, owing to its Semitic traditions, had little figure-sculpture of any sort. We are thrown back, therefore, on the terra-incognita of Asia Minor. Here, if anywhere, such sculpture was possible; in late Imperial times it had a sculptural school of no mean order, and Strzygowski has shown that Armenia had some centuries later a vigorous figure-sculpture which he himself compares with that of the Northumbrian crosses.[1] It has, however, yet to be shown that Armenia, Anatolia, or indeed any part of hither Asia produced such work in the seventh century, and until excavation proves or disproves its existence it is useless to pursue the subject.

The later development of figure-sculpture is best studied in the midlands. In Northumbria it declined rapidly in the second half of the eighth century and never recovered throughout the Saxon period. In Mercia, however, a certain level was maintained throughout the period of that kingdom's supremacy, but it never attained the quality of the earlier work either in the south or the north. The best examples are at Castor (Northants.),[2] Peterborough [3] (the Hedda Stone) (Pl. 30), Fletton [4] (Hunts.), Breedon [4]

---

[1] J. Strzygowski, *The Origins of Christian Church Art.*
[2] *Antiq. Journ.*, iv, p. 421, and *Archaeologia*, lxxvii, p. 236.
[3] *Archaeologia*, lxxiv, p. 238. [4] *Ibid.*, lxxvii, pp. 233 et seq.

(Leicestershire) (Pl. 60), Bradbourne (Derbyshire) (Pl. 18), and Stapleford (Notts.). Of these perhaps the best is the stone with two figures at Breedon, where the drapery has a freedom which is not present in the Peterborough group. Some of the sculpture at Bradbourne has perhaps traces of greater power, but the stones are too weathered for a just appreciation.

It is, however, in certain details of this midland carving that its chief interest lies. We find here the use of a number of conventions which are of the greatest value in fixing its approximate date. Thus at Breedon the two large figures (Pl. 60) are represented giving the blessing in the Greek manner, at Stapleford (Notts.), Ilkley[1] (Yorks.) (Fig. 17), Wirksworth[2] (Derby) (Pl. 22), and probably Edenham[3] (Lincs.) (Pl. 21) we find three Evangelists represented as human figures with beasts' heads, and at Bishop Auckland (Durham) (Pl. 21), Bradbourne, Sheffield (now in the Brit. Mus.) (Fig. 18),[4] and elsewhere are archers carved at the base of the shafts, shooting at the birds and beasts above. All of these unusual conventions or motives are illustrated in contemporary manuscripts. The Greek blessing appears in two English manuscripts (Pl. 23) of the latter part of the eighth and in Carolingian manuscripts of the first half of the ninth century.[5] The human-beast figures of Evangelists make a nearly contemporary appearance in one English (Pl. 24) and two French manuscripts, all of the latter part of the eighth century.[6] The figure of an archer, shooting at birds in scrolled foliage above (as in the English crosses),

---

[1] *Yorks. Arch. Journ.*, xxiii, p. 187.

[2] *Rivista di Arch. Cristiana*, 1924, p. 149. The scenes represent, according to Marucchi: (1) the washing of the disciples' feet; (2) the crucifixion symbolically represented; (3) the bearing of the Body to burial, with the souls in limbo above; (4) the three women at the sepulchre; (5) the ascension; (6) Peter in prison and his departure from Joppa. Scenes (3) and (6) are highly unusual, if not unique, in early Christian art.

[3] *Arch. Journ.*, lxxxiii, p. 13.   [4] *Yorks. Arch. Journ.*, xxiii, p. 238.

[5] See list of examples in *Archaeologia*, lxxvii, p. 234 note.

[6] Vatican Gospels (Barb. Lat. 570), Laon Orosius and Sacramentary of Gellone, all illustrated in Zimmerman, *Vorkarolingische Miniaturen*.

FIG. 17. Ilkley, Cross-shaft.

FIG. 18. Sheffield, Cross-shaft.

appears in the Psalter of Corbie [1] (Pl. 23) assigned to the beginning of the ninth century. It will thus be seen that there
is very strong external evidence for the placing of all these
sculptures within the period 750–850, for the dating of
the manuscripts rests on a far surer basis than that of
the sculptures.

Side by side with the human figures the later stone-
carvers of the middle and south of England began to make
use of a beast which at first was a direct borrowing from
Northumbrian art (Pls. 25, 27). The Anglian Beast
(Pls. 16, 19), as Professor Brøndsted has named it, early
made its appearance in the north, and survived there
throughout the pre-Danish period and beyond. At Breedon
(Leicestershire) it forms one of the staple motives of the
great series of friezes, to which we shall presently return,
but towards the close of the period, i.e. the middle and
second half of the ninth century, it gave place to a very
different type of beast. This animal has been derived from
the pairs of beasts commonly represented on Merovingian
manuscripts of the eighth century, and copied in English
manuscripts of the end of that century. It makes a somewhat uncommon appearance in stone-carving, but is well
represented on the cross-shaft recently found at Breedon
(Pl. 29) and is repeated with later features at Gloucester
and Derby. The shaft at Gloucester is assigned by Brøndsted to the end of the ninth century, and that at Breedon
is perhaps a generation earlier.

Before leaving the subject of Mercian carving it will be
well to consider the few remains of structural and ritual
ornament which survive. We cannot doubt that in the
seventh- and eighth-century English churches some attempt
was made to copy the decoration and ornaments of the
contemporary churches of Italy and Gaul. Prior Richard
of Hexham records that, in that church, St. Wilfrid
adorned the walls and the 'capitals of the columns that

---

[1] Illustrated in A. Boinet, *La Miniature Carolingienne*, Pl. 159.

PLATE 21

BISHOP AUCKLAND,
DURHAM, CROSS-SHAFT
8th century

EDENHAM, LINCS., CROSS-SHAFT,
ST. JOHN (?)
8th century

PLATE 22

WIRKSWORTH, DERBYSHIRE, TOMB-SLAB

8th century

sustain them and the arch of the sanctuary with designs and images and with many sculptured figures in relief on the stone and pictures with a pleasing variety of colours and a wonderful charm'.[1] Eddius speaks of the hangings of purple and silk provided by Wilfrid, and the ornaments of gold and silver and precious stones added by Acca to the same structure. Alcuin, in his description of the church at York, makes mention of *egregii laqueares*, which Baldwin Brown renders 'splendid coffered ceilings'. Benedict Biscop's church at Monkwearmouth contained a series of paintings,[2] and above the door of the porch there still remain traces of a carved frieze and a sculptured figure, perhaps a Christ. At Glastonbury, William of Malmesbury records[3] that the pavement of the *vetusta ecclesia* was inlaid with polished stone in which were, on every side, stones designedly interlaid with triangles and squares and set with lead. It is possible, however, that this pavement belonged to the succeeding (Carolingian) period.

We have thus some indication of the internal decoration of the English churches of the early period, and it will be noted that no mention is made of wall-mosaics. This is not surprising in view of the fact that there is but one example, and this of the beginning of the ninth century, in France.

Of the few surviving relics of this internal decoration the foremost place is taken by the remarkable series of carved friezes at Breedon on the Hill (Pls. 25–7).[4] Here there

[1] Twysden, *Decem Scriptores* (1652), i, chap. iii: 'Ipsos (muros) etiam et capitella columnarum quibus sustentantur et arcum sanctuarii historiis et imaginibus et variis celaturarum figuris ex lapide prominentibus et picturarum et colorum grata varietate mirabilique decore decoravit.' The translation is Baldwin Brown's.
[2] Bede, *Hist. Abbatum* (Plummer's edition), i, p. 368.
[3] *Gesta Regum Anglorum* (Rolls Ser.), i, p. 24: 'Adeo pavimentum lapide polito crustatum adeo altaris latera, ipsumque altare, supra et infra, reliquiis confertissimis aggeruntur. Ubi etiam notare licet in pavimento, vel per triangulum vel per quadratum, lapides altrinsecus ex industria positos et plumbo sigillatos.'
[4] A. W. Clapham, 'The Carved Stones at Breedon on the Hill', in *Archaeologia*, lxxvii, p. 219. In a private letter, dated 6th June 1928, Professor J. Brøndsted expressed entire agreement with the conclusions arrived at in this paper.

still exists some sixty feet of carved ornament, consisting of ivy-vine scrolls, human, beast, and bird figures in considerable variety, and a number of panels of geometrical ornament. The whole of this ornament can most reasonably be placed in the latter part of the eighth century, and may serve to show the quality and quantity of the carved enrichment of a church in the most flourishing period of the Mercian kingdom. A few lengths of very similar frieze-panels remain at Fletton (Hunts.), and almost certainly come from the neighbouring abbey of Peterborough. The precise position of such friezes in a church is difficult to determine, but that they were internal is proved by the excellent preservation of most of the carving. The few other surviving fragments of church-sculpture belong rather to the ritual than the structural part of the building. It is probable that, as in Italy, the choirs of the priests and the singers were partitioned off by stone cancelli or low screens, and the fragments of late seventh- or early eighth-century carved panels (Pl. 28) at South Kyme (Lincolnshire) may well have served such a purpose. That the choir of the priests consisted of a series of benches round the apse with the seat of the head of the house in the middle is rendered likely by the survival of portions of the bench, in this position, at Reculver; and the stone seats preserved at Hexham (Pl. 30) and Beverley may well be the early bishop's or abbot's stools of those places. The carved frieze and the panel with figures at Hovingham (Yorks.) most probably formed the reredos of an altar, and the same may have been the purpose of some of the slabs with figure-sculpture at Breedon, Castor, and Fletton.

It remains only to consider the forms adopted for the memorials to the dead, apart from the high crosses which only occasionally served this purpose. The humbler memorials are almost all small stone slabs, or stelae, carved with a more or less elaborate cross and generally bearing the name of the deceased either in runes or in Irish capitals

PLATE 23

STOCKHOLM CODEX AUREUS, S. ENGLISH,
ST. JOHN
late 8th century

PSALTER OF CORBIE, ARCHER AND
BIRDS
early 9th century

PLATE 24

VATICAN GOSPELS (BARB. LAT. 570), S. ENGLISH, COMPOSITE FIGURES
OF EVANGELISTS

late 8th century

or in both. Of these slabs there survives a considerable number, of which the majority are grouped on the sites of the monasteries of Lindisfarne (Pl. 20)[1] and Hartlepool.[2] They were formerly called 'pillow-stones', on the assumption that they were placed under the head of the body, but it is now generally agreed that they were placed flat upon the grave and that the 'pillow-stone' proper was commonly uncarved. These English stones are very closely paralleled by a number of Irish examples, three of which, at Clonmacnois, are satisfactorily dated to about the years 890, 950, and 994;[3] and it has consequently been argued that the English examples, equating with the later Irish ones, must be of this date also. This contention is against all historical probability, as the monasteries of neither Lindisfarne nor Hartlepool survived the end of the ninth century, and there is ample evidence that both in the form of the crosses and in their decoration the English stones are in place in the eighth and ninth centuries but are impossible in the tenth. That the Irish stone-carving should be a century behind the English is not in the least surprising when we consider that in every Celtic country the same phenomenon is observable.

Two other forms of memorial must be noticed before quitting the subject. The first is only represented by a single example at Howell (Lincs.);[4] it is a stone coffin-lid ornamented with a series of raised crosses very similar to those on the Merovingian sarcophagi found within the foundations of the abbey of S. Geneviève, Paris, and elsewhere. That Roman stone coffins were not infrequently

---

[1] C. R. Peers, 'The Inscribed and Sculptured Stones of Lindisfarne', *Archaeologia* lxxiv, p. 255.

[2] G. Baldwin Brown, *The Ruthwell and Bewcastle Crosses*, chaps. ii and iii.

[3] It is significant that the design of these three stones—those of Suibhne mac Mael-Umha, *c.* 890, Dubcenn mac Tadhgain, *c.* 950, and Odran hua Eolais, 994, all at Clonmacnois—are very closely akin, showing that design had changed little in a century; indeed, the latest of these slabs is the simplest of the three and typologically the earliest. See *The Memorial Slabs of Clonmacnois*, R. A. S. Macalister (1909).

[4] Reproduced in *Arch. Journ.*, xxvii, p. 196.

re-used for Saxon interments is shown by the survival of one at Westminster Abbey, with a cross cut on the lid, and by the story that the monks of Ely went to Grantchester to find a Roman coffin in which to bury the body of St. Etheldreda. Abbot Adrian for long lay in a marble coffin, richly adorned, at St. Augustine's, Canterbury, and this also was probably of Roman provenance.

The second special type of memorial is exemplified in the Hedda Stone (Pl. 30) at Peterborough. This is a solid block in the form of a small chest with a gabled roof, and is enriched with a series of figures on the sides and birds and interlace on the top. According to the Peterborough tradition, preserved in the Pseudo-Ingulph, it covered the remains of the monks martyred by the Danes and stood in the cemetery. Its decoration indicates that it belongs rather to the second half of the eighth century. A fragment of a similar stone is preserved in the church of Bakewell (Derbyshire).

Chapter IV

CAROLINGIAN ARCHITECTURE IN ENGLAND

THE establishment of the Carolingian Empire created a
new era in European art as it did in European history
The cohesion which it gave to western Europe, shadowy and
ephemeral as it was, was reflected in a corresponding
artistic cohesion which outgrew and outlived the political
structure of Charlemagne and his house and extended into
lands which never formed part of his empire. We should
not be far wrong in assuming that ecclesiastical art and
architecture in England from the ninth century to the eve
of the Conquest was a direct offshoot of the Carolingian
stem, guarding the salient characteristics of its parent stock
until the advent of the Normans put a sudden stop to its
growth and its life together. It is often assumed that Saxon
architecture was a poor stunted growth, without the seeds
of expansion, and that we owe to the Normans our rescue
from an artistic stagnation out of which it was vain to hope
for salvation. Recent research, on the contrary, has gone
far to prove that in the minor arts the Norman conquest
was little short of a catastrophe, blotting out alike a good
tradition and an accomplished execution, and setting in
its place a semi-barbaric art which attempted little and did
that little ill. In the major art of architecture it is not un-
reasonable to suppose that, left to themselves, the Saxons
would have travelled along the same road as their Rhineland kinsmen and, given peace and prosperity, would have
produced an architecture not unlike the Carolingian
Romanesque of the great cathedrals and abbey churches of
that province, retaining many of the marks of its parentage,
and assimilating such features of the rival styles of northern
France as were found to improve upon its construction or
enhance its effect. As it was, the greater Saxon churches

of the tenth and eleventh centuries, though lacking the scale of their continental contemporaries, were probably not unworthy to survive, and in every other direction were quite up to the standards of the age.

It is unfortunate for the history of English architecture that almost without exception these greater churches have perished without leaving a trace; and it is only by collating the scattered documentary evidence that some idea can be arrived at as to their disposition and ornament. It will be well first to consider this evidence and compare it with the far fuller evidence, both architectural and literary, supplied by continental examples, for only by so doing can a just estimate be formed of the value and characteristics of the English Carolingian style. The study of the surviving examples alone, which in the nature of the case are commonly remote and undistinguished village churches, can only lead to a one-sided and very partial realization of the facts; it will prove of great value for the minutiae of the subject, the details of construction and ornament, but the main features of the picture will necessarily be largely untouched and unillustrated. The architectural achievement of any age must be judged by the standard of the principal buildings of that age and not by that of the obscure and the second rate. We shall be justified then in considering the main characteristics of the Carolingian churches of the Continent if it can be shown that these characteristics were equally represented in the English churches, and this, I think, can be proved beyond all cavil. It is fortunate that one of the nearest of the great Carolingian churches, S. Riquier in Picardy, has been the subject of a masterly monograph [1] by M. G. Durand, and this provides the fullest and most complete account of such a church which is at present available. A short consideration of its salient features will form the best introductory to a study of the corresponding records of English churches.

[1] G. Durand, 'S. Riquier', in *La Picardie historique et monumentale*, iv (1911).

PLATE 25

BREEDON ON THE HILL, LEICESTERSHIRE, FRIEZE-PANELS

late 8th century

PLATE 26

BREEDON, LEICESTERSHIRE, PANEL OF PELTA-ORNAMENT

late 8th century

BREEDON, LEICESTERSHIRE, FRIEZE-PANEL

late 8th century

The new church of S. Riquier, then called Centula (Fig. 19), was begun by Abbot Angilbert about 790, and subsisted in great part until it was again rebuilt about 1090. The accompanying plan, adapted from that of M. Durand, is deduced from documentary sources and from reproductions of a drawing (Fig. 20) made before the rebuilding at the end of the eleventh century. All the details shown upon it are amply documented by M. Durand, and the

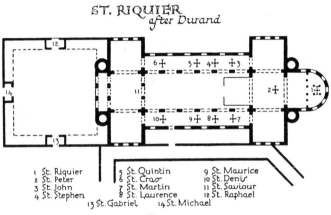

ST. RIQUIER
after Durand

1 St. Riquier	5 St. Quintin	9 St. Maurice
2 St. Peter	6 St. Cross	10 St. Denis
3 St. John	7 St. Martin	11 St. Saviour
4 St. Stephen	8 St. Laurence	12 St. Raphael
13 St. Gabriel	14 St. Michael	

FIG. 19.

only uncertain elements are the scale and exact proportions. The church was of cruciform plan, with a second transept at the west end, and a presbytery and apse, projecting east of the eastern transept. Above each crossing rose a round or octagonal tower having open arcaded stages, each stage set back from the faces of the stage below. Flanking the presbytery and at the west end of the church were four round towers containing spiral staircases (*cochleae*). The body of the church was six bays long and had side aisles and a clearstorey of large round-headed windows; windows of like form lighted the apse, presbytery, and aisles. The ends of the transepts had three ranges of windows, those of the middle range being of circular form; there was, perhaps, also an upper range of circular windows in the presbytery. Inside the church there was apparently no triforium, but

FIG. 20.   S. Riquier, Picardy, before 1090.

between the arcades and the clearstorey ran a projecting gallery, resting on stone corbelling, in the form of machico-lations,[1] and having some sort of a parapet on the outer side. Beneath the west tower, and possibly extending to the whole of the west transept, was a gallery supported on vaults which permitted free ingress from the west doorways to the body of the church. To the west of the church was an open forecourt or 'Paradise' with an entrance tower on each free side, called after the three chief archangels. Surrounding the forecourt, probably from the time of Angilbert, were roofed galleries, and covering the west doorways of the church was a portico or narthex.

The ritual arrangements of the church were elaborate and richly decorated. There were three chief altars, that of S. Riquier in the apse, that of St. Peter under the eastern crossing, and that of St. Saviour on the gallery under the western crossing; each of these altars had a gold and silver 'table' in front and was surmounted by a *ciborium* from which hung a crown. In front of the altar of S. Riquier were six columns of bronze supporting a cross-beam on which stood thirteen shrines. Eight side altars occupied the two aisles of the nave. There appear to have been four choirs: (*a*) that of the religious, at the east end of the struc-tural nave; (*b*) in the 'throne' of S. Riquier, towards the west, apparently under the eastern crossing; (*c*) in the apse (*buticum*); (*d*) at the altar of St. Saviour, on the western gallery. The marble columns and wall-facings of the church were brought from Italy, as no doubt was also the marble paving of *opus Alexandrinum*, which covered the eastern parts of the church. The wall-face on the west side of the eastern tower, fronting the nave, was covered with a stucco relief of the Crucifixion; similar reliefs of the Resurrection and the Ascension decorated the adjoining north and south walls of the nave, and there was a fourth relief of the Nativity in the narthex, above the western

---

[1] Cf. the late twelfth- or thirteenth-century cathedral of Ruvo, Italy.

doorways of the church. S. Riquier and the two Irish missionaries, first founders of the church of Centula, were buried in the presbytery, and Angilbert, builder of the church, was buried outside the west doors, so that his tomb might be trodden by those entering and leaving the church.

Such in broad outline was the structure and decoration of the church of S. Riquier. Let us now examine the various features which appear to distinguish it as a building of the Carolingian age and differentiate it from the earlier and

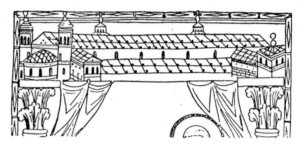

Fig. 21.   The Carolingian Cathedral of Cologne.

later types of church-building. In the first place the most distinctive feature of the plan is the double transept, with the second cross-arm at the west end of the church. This feature was represented also in the Carolingian cathedral at Cologne (Fig. 21), of which a miniature representation survives, and was no doubt fairly common in the larger churches of the period. It persisted down to the twelfth century at least in that stronghold of Carolingian tradition, the Rhine district, and is exemplified at the cathedral of Speyer, at Munster, and elsewhere. Within the modern limits of France are a few churches still preserving the same tradition, including the cathedral of Verdun, and there is a western apse and transept at Besançon and Nevers.

The second point to be noticed is the form and position of the towers. Their form, a series of receding stages of open arcading, can hardly have been executed, at that time, in any other material than timber, at any rate in their upper part, and this is borne out both by the documentary evidence of other buildings of the same epoch and also by the structural evidence of such Carolingian buildings as survive. The tower at Fontenelle (S. Wandrille), built by Ansegis in 833, is described [1] as a square pyramid of timber 35 ft. high. The description [2] of the tower built in 860 at S. Bertin, S. Omer, implies the same thing, as it is mentioned that when *laid out on the ground* it equalled the full height of the church on which it was to be placed. The surviving Carolingian crossings at S. Philbert de Grandlieu [3] (Déols) and at S. Martin d'Angers [4] are manifestly insufficient to support anything more substantial than a timber super-structure. Having regard to the subsequent devastations of the Normans and to the perishable nature of the material it is not surprising that none of these towers now survives, but representations of a few have been preserved in manu-scripts. The drawing of the cathedral at Cologne, already referred to, shows two towers exhibiting the same receding and arcaded stages as at S. Riquier, and there is also an early drawing (Pl. 31*b*) of the cathedral at Chartres [5] showing two similar features. The early thirteenth-century seal (Pl. 31*c*) of the chapter of Chichester provides a third ex-ample; it matters little to our purpose if this is copied from an earlier seal or drawing, and represents the Saxon cathe-dral at Selsey or the Saxon minster at Chichester. One thing is obvious—that we are here presented with a delinea-

---

[1] *Gesta abbatum Fontanellensium, Mon. Germ. S.S.*, ii, p. 296: 'pyramidem quad-rangulam altitudinis triginta quinque pedum de ligno tornatili compositam in culmine turris ejusdem ecclesiae.'

[2] *Acta Sanctorum O.S.B.*, iii, p. 129: ' Sed et turrile ipsius licet noviter esset superpositum, quia antiquo more erat factum, deposuerunt, et aliud mirae magnitudinis fabricae studuerunt aedificare, cujus longitudo consistentis in terra aequabat altitudinem culminis ecclesiae cui superponendum erat. Nec mirum, tristegum enim trium tripodum ordinibus factum fuerat excepta summa claxendice.'

[3] Lasteyrie, *Mém. Acad. des Inscriptions et Belles-Lettres*, xxxviii.

[4] *Congrès archéologique de France* (Angers), i. 198.

[5] Of early eleventh-century date, reproduced in Clairval and Merlet, *Un Manuscrit Chartrain.*

tion of just such a tower as formerly existed at Cologne and S. Riquier. The tradition of this form of tower, translated into stone, is again well preserved in the later Romanesque churches of the Rhine valley, where they form a distinctive feature of the local style.

The position of the two towers of S. Riquier, placed axially over the east and west parts of the church, is a very distinctive feature which, so far as I am aware, is not to be found in any church before the Carolingian period. It has left its mark, however, very deeply on the Rhine provinces, where many of the greater Romanesque churches follow this form, and more lightly on the less central parts of Charlemagne's empire. The eleventh-century church at Fleury (S. Benôit sur Loire) no doubt followed the tradition of its Carolingian predecessor, and other examples might be cited at Limoges, S. Savin, and elsewhere. The very general adoption of the practice in England will be dealt with later.

Passing now to the interior of the church, the most unusual feature is the raised gallery at the west end, on which stood the Saviour's altar and choir. M. Durand has collected evidence of the wide popularity of altars with this dedication, at the period, and cites texts describing a precisely similar structure [1] at Reims Cathedral begun in 816; this gallery was taken down by Archbishop Adalbéron, in 976, to enlarge the nave. The position of an altar at the west end of the nave is bound up with another very general peculiarity of Carolingian churches, the double-apse plan— that is to say, the plan exhibiting an apse at both ends of the church. This feature was not present at S. Riquier but is shown on the early ninth-century plan of St. Gall,[2] and existed in the early cathedral at Cologne and in numerous

[1] *Mon. Germ. S.S.*, iii, p. 407: 'arcuatum opus quod erat secus valvas ecclesiae sanctae Mariae Remensis supra quod altare Sancti Salvatoris habebatur et fontes miro opere erant positi.'

[2] R. Willis, 'Description of the Ancient Plan of the Monastery of St. Gall', *Arch. Journ.*, v, p. 85, and often reproduced.

PLATE 27

BREEDON, LEICESTERSHIRE, FRIEZE-PANELS

late 8th century

PLATE 28

BREEDON, LEICESTERSHIRE, FRIEZE-PANEL
late 8th century

SOUTH KYME, LINCS., FRAGMENTS
late 7th or early 8th century

PLATE 29

NORBURY, DERBY, CROSS-SHAFT
late 9th or 10th century

BREEDON, LEICESTERSHIRE, CROSS-SHAFT
late 9th century

PLATE 30

HEXHAM, NORTHUMBERLAND, FRITH STOOL
late 7th or early 8th century

PETERBOROUGH, NORTHANTS., 'HEDDA'S STONE'
late 8th century

Romanesque churches both in Germany and France that derive from the Carolingian tradition. We have already seen that this plan makes an earlier appearance in England (at Abingdon) and have suggested a possible origin for the type.

Two other points in the structure of the church at S. Riquier must be noticed, of which the most prominent is the number and form of the staircase towers. These were circular externally and contained spiral staircases (*cochleae*). They form one of the most noticeable features of Carolingian architecture, and are well exemplified on the St. Gall plan, in the Minster at Aachen (Fig. 47), and in numerous other churches of the same and a later age. The windows at S. Riquier were of comparatively large size, generally round-headed and sometimes circular. This last was a favourite form in churches of the period. It occurs in surviving examples at S. Jean, Poitiers, and Jumièges (as panels), and is shown on the miniatures of Cologne Cathedral and Echternach (Pl. 31 *a*).

We must now turn to consider how far the features we have been considering were reflected in the greater English churches of which any record survives. Such records, all more or less fragmentary, are available for the cathedrals of Canterbury, Winchester, and Durham, and the abbeys of Ely, Ramsey, Thorney, and Glastonbury. In addition to these there are surviving remains of the cathedral of Elmham and the minsters at Peterborough, Deerhurst, and St. Augustine, Canterbury. The details of each of these must be considered in turn before the general comparison can be proceeded with.

(*a*) *Canterbury.* A description of the building before its destruction by fire in 1067 is given by Edmer the Precentor.[1] This building has been thought to have preserved portions of the Roman church restored by St. Augustine and of St. Augustine's own building. This, however, is largely

[1] *Gervase of Canterbury* (Rolls Ser.), i, p. 7.

conjecture, and the building as it stood at the Norman Conquest must have been in form and arrangement rather a monument of the restoration of Archbishop Odo (940–60) than of any earlier age. The church, according to Edmer, consisted of a body (*aula*) with aisles and two towers standing about half-way down and above (*ultra*) the aisles. The southern tower formed a porch and contained an altar of St. Gregory; the corresponding tower on the north was dedicated to St. Martin and was surrounded by the cloister. At the east end of the presbytery, which appears to have been apsidal, was the high altar dedicated to Christ. This portion of the church was raised many steps above the body of the building, and under it was a crypt or *confessio*. Immediately west of the crypt wall was the tomb of St. Dunstan with the morrow-mass altar at his head. Thence towards the west extended the choir of the singers, shut off by an enclosure from the public part of the nave. At the extreme west end of the building was a raised platform on which stood the altar of St. Mary and behind it, against the west wall, was the bishop's throne.

This description has been the subject of several essays at elucidation, notably those of Professor Willis [1] and Sir William Hope.[2] Both of these writers have sought to differentiate the work of the Romans and that of St. Augustine, but their theories have both been based upon the assumption that the two towers marked the junction of the two works. Now such structures are unusual, not to say impossible, at both suggested dates; whereas the twin flanking chapels or porticus are, as we have shown in a previous chapter, a distinctive mark of the early Kentish type of church; the dedications to St. Martin and St. Gregory also point very decidedly to this date and purpose, and are exactly paralleled by chapels with the same dedications at St. Augustine's

[1] R. Willis, *Architectural History of Canterbury Cathedral*.
[2] 'The Plan and Arrangement of the first Cathedral Church of Canterbury', Sir W. St. J. Hope, *Proc. Soc. Ants.*, xxx, p. 137.

Abbey. We have thus very strong evidence that the two towers were originally the projecting porticus of St. Augustine's Cathedral to which towers were added, probably in the tenth century, as they were added over so many other porticus in the same period.[1] Such porticus may have been at the east end of St. Augustine's nave, as in most other instances, or placed mid-way, as at St. Pancras, so that they give little indication of the length or termination of Augustine's church.

It seems probable, though it is not definitely stated, that the church had apses both at the east and west ends, but as to the date of either it would be idle to speculate. It need only be added that Archbishop Cuthbert (741–58) built a baptistery east of the main church and almost touching it.

(b) *Winchester.*[2] Of the early church of Winchester, built by Kings Kynegils and Kynewald, we know very little, as the notice of burials of early bishops in the crypt may be a record of reinterment. St. Swithin (d. 863) was buried before the west door between the nave and a great tower which stood over the entrance to the 'holy temple'. It is, however, again doubtful if this tower was standing in St. Swithin's days. In any case the church itself was very largely rebuilt by Bishop Ethelwold, dedicated in 980, and completed by his successor Alphege. This church is described in a long poem by Wolstan, from which the following information can be extracted. The new building appears to have been longer than the old as a foundation was laid eastward, 'so that a porticus might be there built to the Deity'. Crypts were added under it, of which the roofs and entrances only were visible, and which supported the altar. The church itself had many chapels (oratories) 'intended for those who would ask help of the saints', and a great tower—'in five compartments pierced by open windows,

---

[1] E.g. Monkwearmouth, Brixworth, Corbridge, Bradwell, &c.
[2] R. Willis, 'The Architectural History of Winchester Cathedral', *Proc. Arch. Inst. Winchester* (1845), p. 1.

on all four sides as many ways are open. The lofty peaks of the tower are capped with pointed roofs, and are adorned with various and sinuous vaults, carved with well-skilled contrivance. . . . Above these stands a rod with golden balls and at the top a mighty cock.' Ethelwold also repaired the atria of the old church 'with lofty walls and new roofs and strengthened it on the north sides and on the south sides with solid porticus and various arches'. He added also many buildings (*aedes*) with altars 'to distract attention from the threshold of the church', which was approached by more than one vestibule. From this description it is evident that the church had an arcaded forecourt or atrium, vestibules somewhat similar to those of which remains have been found at St. Augustine's, Canterbury (Fig. 49), a great tower closely resembling the staged towers of the continental examples we have already cited, and a *confessio* similar to that at Canterbury Cathedral.

(*c*) *Durham*. Some particulars of the form of the 'White Church' built by Bishop Aldhun and hallowed in 999 are preserved by Reginald of Durham.[1] He states that there were 'in the White Church . . . two stone towers, as those who saw them have told us, standing high into the air, the one containing the choir, the other standing at the west end of the church, which were of wonderful size. They carried brazen pinnacles set up on top.' It seems evident that the eastern tower stood over a crossing and that the building was thus cruciform.[2]

(*d*) *Elmham*. The cathedral of Elmham (Fig. 22) is almost certainly to be identified with the remarkable structure (Pl. 32) of which considerable remains survive at North

---

[1] Reginald of Durham, chap. xvi (Surtees Soc.), i, p. 29: 'Erant siquidem in Alba Ecclesia, in qua primitus requieverat, duae turres lapideae, sicut qui videre nobis retulere, altius per aera prominentes, altera chorum continens, alia vero in fine ecclesiae occidentali subsistens; quae mirae magnitudinis aerea pinnacula in supremo erecta gestaverant.'

[2] A reconstruction of the plan has been attempted by Sir Wm. Hope in *Proc. Soc. Ants.*, xxii, p. 416.

PLATE 31

a. Echternach Abbey (Luxemburg)

b. Chartres Cathedral

c. Chichester Cathedral seal

REPRESENTATIONS OF CHURCHES OF THE
CAROLINGIAN TYPE

PLATE 32

a. NORTH ELMHAM CATHEDRAL, NORFOLK, NAVE AND
S. TRANSEPT

early 11th century

b. ST. AUGUSTINE'S ABBEY, CANTERBURY, WULFRIC'S
ROTUNDA

mid 11th century

Elmham, Norfolk.[1] There is no documentary evidence of the date of its building, but the general features point to a date either late in the tenth or early in the eleventh century. The church consisted of an aisleless nave, a T-shaped transept with a shallow apse projecting from its eastern face, a large tower at the west end, and two small towers

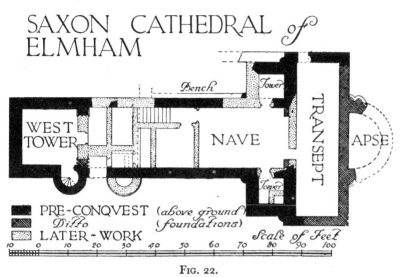

SAXON CATHEDRAL of ELMHAM

WEST TOWER — NAVE — TRANSEPT — APSE

Bench — Tower — Tower

PRE-CONQVEST (above ground)
Ditto (foundations)
LATER-WORK

Scale of Feet

FIG. 22.

in the angles between the transept and nave. The whole structure is built almost entirely of conglomerate, and possesses a remarkable decorative feature in the curious semi-cylindrical buttresses or piers which occupy the re-entrant angles of the building and surrounded the apse. It may be surmised that the two smaller towers contained staircases. The church had a total internal length of 123 ft., its small size being due, no doubt, partly to the depressed state of East Anglia after the Danish invasions and partly to the lack of building-stone in the district.

(*e*) *Ely.* No description exists of the church built or restored at Ely by Ethelwold, but two casual references

[1] A. W. Clapham and W. H. Godfrey, 'The Saxon Cathedral of Elmham', *Antiq. Journ.*, vi, p. 402.

throw some light on the building. A poem in the Anglo-Saxon Chronicle [1] mentions that the burial of the Aetheling Alfred, 1036, at Ely, was 'low in the sacred earth, to the steeple full nigh in the south aisle to lie of the transept west'. It is evident that here there was something very like the plan of the western parts of the church at S. Riquier. It is elsewhere recorded [2] that Leofwin, under Abbot Elsin (981–1016), rebuilt and enlarged the south aisle, joining it to the rest of the building; in one porticus he built an altar to the Blessed Virgin.

(*f*) *Ramsey.* The chronicle of Ramsey Abbey [3] relates that the church built by Ailwin the founder, about 970, had two towers rising above the roof, the smaller being at the west end of the church and the larger standing over the crossing and supported on four columns and arches. Shortly after its erection this tower cracked from top to bottom and had to be rebuilt. Here we have evidently a cruciform church with axial towers.

(*g*) *Thorney.* One of the churches built by Ethelwold of Winchester about 972. The charter of King Edgar [4] states that the bishop dedicated the presbytery and the eastern altar to the Virgin, consecrated the western part of the church to St. Peter and the north porticus to Benedict, 'the patron of all monks'. This would seem to be some indica-

---

[1] Anglo-Saxon Chron., sub anno 1036.

[2] *Liber Eliensis* (Anglia Christiana), i, p. 178 : 'Muros ecclesiae dilatare et ad australem plagam ampliare incoepit et suis expensis reliquo operi unitos consummavit."

[3] *Chronicon Abbatiae Rameseiensis* (Rolls Series), pp. 38 f.: 'Duae quoque turres ipsis tectorum culminibus eminebant quarum minor versus occidentem in fronte basilicae pulchrum intrantibus insulam a longe spectaculum praebebat; major vero in quadrifidae structurae medio columnas quatuor porrectis de alia ad aliam arcubus sibi invicem connexas ne laxe defluerent deprimebat.' An account of the same church occurs in the 'Life of Bishop Oswald', *Historians of the Church of York* (Rolls Ser.), i, p. 434.

[4] Dugdale, *Mon. Ang.* ii (1819), p. 599: 'Dei scilicet genetrici semperque Virgini Mariae orientale altaris presbiterium dedicans, occidentalem vero cleri et populi ejusdem ecclesiae partem beato Petro, regni coelorum clavigero, necnon aquilonarem ipsius basilicae porticum beato Benedicto, omnium monachorum patrono, consecravit.'

tion of altars at both ends of the church though it can hardly be taken to prove the existence of a double-apse plan.

(*h*) *Peterborough.* Parts of the walls of the church rebuilt by Ethelwold in 970–2 have been discovered under the nave and south transept of the present cathedral.[1] They contain re-used material, and so can hardly be of earlier date. The plan included a transept 86 ft. by 34 ft. with a small presbytery, 23 ft. wide, projecting towards the east. The termination of this arm, though probably square, is uncertain, as are the dimensions and form of the nave. There are no surviving indications of a tower over the crossing, but the internal angles of the chancel had been robbed of their responds. The walls have a uniform thickness of 2 ft. 9 in., and there are traces of an altar against the east wall of the south transept.

(*i*) *Glastonbury.* Our knowledge of the late Saxon church at Glastonbury is limited to two references, one in Malmesbury's life of St. Dunstan,[2] in which he states that Dunstan lengthened considerably Ine's church and added a tower and aisles or porticus (*alas vel porticus*). The second reference is in the same author's *Antiquity of the Church of Glastonbury.*[3] In relating the circumstances of the quarrel between Abbot Turstin and his monks he mentions that the servants of the abbot, having pursued the monks into the church, ascended into 'an upper chamber constructed between the columns' to shoot down upon their victims. There seems to be little doubt that this entry refers to the old church and not to that which the abbot was then building, and may be taken as evidence that the church as reconstructed by Dunstan had chambers above the porticus.

The recent excavations (1928–9) have revealed the remains of Dunstan's additions. He built a chancel (21 ft. by 17 ft.), perhaps surmounted by a tower, and added

---

[1] J. T. Irvine, 'Account of the discovery of part of the Saxon Abbey Church of Peterborough', *Brit. Arch. Assoc. Journ.*, l, p. 45.

[2] *Memorials of St. Dunstan* (Rolls Ser.), p. 271.

[3] Gale, *Hist. Angl. Script.*, iii, p. 332.

rectangular chapels to the north and south of it (Fig. 16). Within this chancel was a small crypt of earlier date.

(*j*) *Deerhurst*.[1] (Fig. 23.) Whatever may be the opinion as to the date of certain adjuncts of the church at Deerhurst (Pl. 33), there can be no doubt that the building as it stands is mainly a monument of the tenth century. It consists of an aisleless nave with a square 'crossing'[2] at the east end (of this the western arch has been removed), the remains of a presbytery with a polygonal apse, transeptal chapels to the north and south of the crossing, and a western tower of oblong plan. Three features demand special attention: (*a*) the form of the apse, which is polygonal both inside and out, and has pilaster strips at the angles; (*b*) the size of the crossing, which with its thin walls seems designed to carry a timber superstructure; and (*c*) the evidences of the existence of a timber gallery across the western part of the nave (Pl. 34), approached by the still existing doorway in the tower, and supported by the corbels in the side-walls. The form and subdivision of the tower and other features will be referred to in a subsequent chapter.

(*k*) *St. Augustine's Abbey, Canterbury*. The additions to this building which can be with certainty ascribed to this period are the two western vestibules (Fig. 49) added in front of the church and the great rotunda of Abbot Wulfric, which will early be considered with other buildings, of the central type of plan, on a subsequent page.

The foregoing eleven buildings represent the only examples of churches of the first rank of which any considerable evidence of structure is forthcoming, either from existing remains or documentary sources. We must now consider how far they exemplify the characteristics of the continental examples of Carolingian building, and in this discussion a certain number of English buildings of secondary rank will be found further to illustrate the comparison.

---

[1] W. H. Knowles, 'Deerhurst Priory Church', in *Archaeologia*, lxxvii, p. 141.
[2] This was represented by a raised roof until the restorations of the last century.

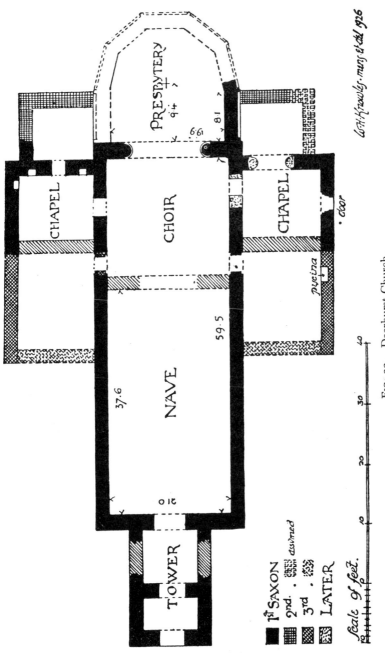

TOWER

NAVE 37.6

210

59.5

CHOIR

CHAPEL

CHAPEL

door

piscina

PRESBYTERY 9.4 ✝

6.6

8.1

1st SAXON
2nd. ▨ assumed
3rd. ▩
LATER ▨

Scale of feet
10 20 30 40

W.H.Knowles mens et del 1926

Fig. 23. Deerhurst Church.

The subject will be best approached under the headings of (a) General Plan, (b) Towers, and (c) Subsidiary Structures. Crypts will be reserved for separate consideration.

(a) The *General Plan* of the larger Carolingian churches may be said in one form or another to be motived by the almost equal importance of the two ends of the building. In this it differs radically from the plan of the corresponding Romanesque churches of the succeeding age, where the nave serves only, or largely, for processional display, and was of such minor importance that it was often not completed until after a period more or less prolonged.[1] Perhaps the most usual form employed to provide for this ritual use was the double-apse plan which, as we have seen, was an ordinary form (perhaps inherited from an earlier tradition) in the Carolingian churches on the Continent and at a still later date in the Rhineland. So far no structural remains of such a building have been found in England,[2] but it is more than probable that this was the form of the cathedral at Canterbury; the general Carolingian practice of having an altar at both ends of the church was certainly exemplified here and also at Thorney. The double cruciform plan with the second transept at the west end was also reproduced in this country at Ely, and, curiously enough, seems to have been copied by the twelfth-century rebuilders in the existing west front.

Bound up with the importance assigned to the west end of the church is the curious feature, exemplified at S. Riquier, Reims, &c., of the western gallery with an altar, commonly dedicated to the Saviour. It seems probable that this contrivance was most commonly used when the west front was the main point of ingress to the church, and not when the double apse was adopted. It provides an excellent explanation of the evidences of a timber gallery in this position at Deerhurst, and there are traces of a similar

---

[1] Cf. Westminster (Confessor's Church), Hereford Cathedral, Durham, &c.

[2] Except the much later little church at Langford, Essex (twelfth century).

arrangement inserted in the earlier work at Brixworth and also at Bosham (Sussex) and Dover, St. Mary's. The main entrance at the west end was thus left free and the required space for the western altar provided in the gallery.[1]

Though not exemplifying any particular Carolingian affinities, a few remarks may here be made on the form of

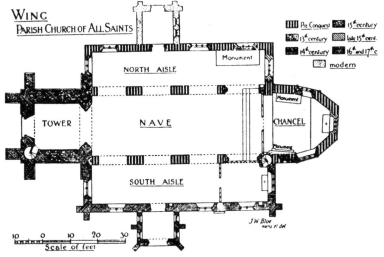

WING
PARISH CHURCH OF ALL SAINTS

⫿⫿⫿ Pre Conquest · 15ᵗʰ century
13ᵗʰ century · late 15ᵗʰ cent.
14ᵗʰ century · 16ᵗʰ and 17ᵗʰ c
modern

NORTH AISLE
Monument

TOWER · NAVE · CHANCEL
Monument
Monument

SOUTH AISLE

J W Bloe
mens et del

10   0   10   20   30
Scale of feet

FIG. 24.

the later Saxon apses. This was not a very favourite form in English work of the period, which exhibited a marked preference for the square east end, but the four which survive, in whole or in part, are all worthy of attention. The examples at Wing (Bucks.) (Fig. 24 and Pl. 35) and Deerhurst are alike in form, being polygonal both within and without;[2] in this they differ significantly from the earlier polygonal apses (at Brixworth and Reculver) where the circular form is retained internally, following the tradition of Ravenna. The third example, at Worth (Sussex)

[1] There is a late survival of the practice in the twelfth-century gallery at the west end of the church of Melbourne (Derbyshire).
[2] Remains of an apse of similar form have been found under the choir of Exeter Cathedral, but whether they belong to the Norman church or an earlier Saxon minster is uncertain. Bishop and Prideaux, *The Building . . . of Exeter.*

(Fig. 29 and Pl. 35), is of the ordinary semicircular form and is more important for the study of architectural detail. The apse at North Elmham (Fig. 22) is a curious survival of the shallow form, projecting immediately from the transept and dating, typologically, from the Constantinian age.[1]

(b) The *Towers* form one of the most distinctive features of Carolingian architecture. They are of two types, the major towers built over the crossing and at the west end, and the minor towers containing staircases. The major towers, normally, consisted, as we have seen, of a series of receding stages enriched with open arcading and were commonly built of timber. That such was the form of many of the towers in England admits of little or no doubt, for not only have we the representation of an example in the seal of Chichester and the significant description of the tower at Winchester, but the surviving remains of several other churches are in favour of the former existence of timber superstructures of a similar nature. Such in all probability was the case at Deerhurst, where the crossing is about 20–21 ft. square with walls $2\frac{1}{2}$ ft. thick; the timber superstructure at Breamore (Hants) (Pl. 36) again may well represent a Saxon original,[2] and, lastly, the crossing at Repton seems designed rather for a timber capping than for a masonry tower. On the other hand, in certain circumstances, stone towers were erected over the crossings of English churches of this age; one such survives at St. Mary in Castro, Dover (Pl. 36), another at Norton (Durham), and a third is implied in the already quoted description of the church at Ramsey.

The placing of two towers axially over the church is the

---

[1] Three further apses, perhaps of this period, have been recovered by excavation at Stanley St. Leonard (Gloucestershire), at Romsey Abbey (Hants), and at St. Mary's Church, Shrewsbury. For the first see *Archaeologia*, lxxi, p. 99, for the second *V. C. H., Hants*, iv, p. 460, and the third *Salop Arch. Soc.*, 2nd ser., vi, pp. 358–71.

[2] Compare the roof-covering of the central tower of Canterbury Cathedral, as shown in the twelfth-century plan of the water-works.

PLATE 33

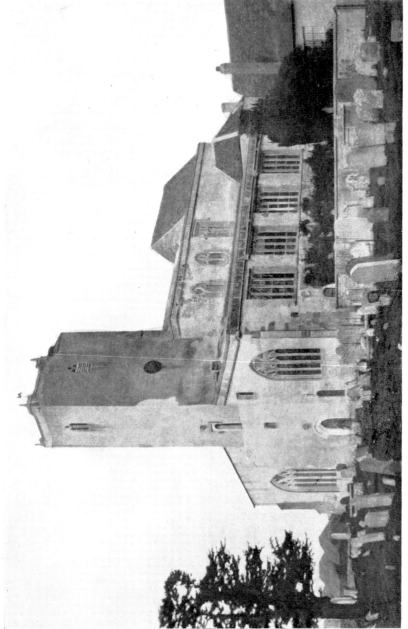

DEERHURST, GLOUCESTERSHIRE, BEFORE RESTORATION

early 10th century

PLATE 34

DEERHURST, GLOUCESTERSHIRE, W. END OF NAVE
early 10th century

Carolingian arrangement most favoured in England. We have seen that it occurred at Durham, Ramsey, and probably at Ely, and its survival in a few English post-Conquest churches [1] is evidence of the tenacity of a tradition that overcame the then prevailing Norman fashion.

The staircase towers of Carolingian churches were commonly circular structures disposed symmetrically near the east or west ends of the churches and unfortunately but few examples have survived in England. The flanking staircase towers of Wulfric's octagon at St. Augustine, Canterbury, are, however, typical examples, and a similar form is preserved in the staircases attached to the major towers at Brixworth, Brigstock, and North Elmham.

We have noted that the two subsidiary towers at the latter place probably also contained staircases, but in this case they are square on plan reflecting the late Saxon aversion from the curved form in building. Here, on the other hand, they occupy a position analogous to that of numerous continental examples in the Carolingian tradition.

(c) *Subsidiary Buildings.* The only subsidiary structure which requires a few words is the atrium. The description of the forecourt at S. Riquier with its three entrance towers well illustrates the scanty references to the atrium at Winchester with its tower over the western entrance, its colonnaded alleys and adjacent chapels. The burial of St. Swithin, here, reflects almost exactly the corresponding burial of Abbot Angilbert in the atrium at S. Riquier. The only other church in England where there is any definite evidence of an atrium is at St. Augustine, Canterbury. Here some traces of the north wall were found and some remains of the tower over the western entrance, which according to the records contained a chapel of St. Mary.

The foregoing remarks will be sufficient to indicate the main features in which the larger English churches followed

---

[1] E. g. Ely, Bury, Winchester, Leominster, and probably Kelso.

the Carolingian model. It now remains to consider in what particulars they departed from it, and how far these departures were due to an earlier tradition or to native predilection.

The aisled church was not, according to most of the indications, a very common form in pre-Conquest England.

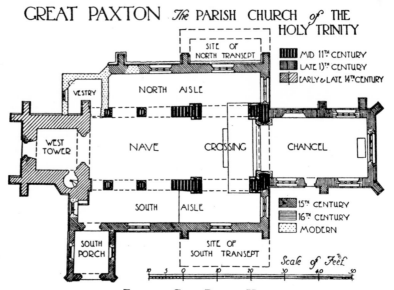

FIG. 25.   Great Paxton, Hunts.

It occurred at Canterbury and in a few smaller churches of the tenth and eleventh centuries, such as Wing[1] (Fig. 24), Great Paxton[2] (Fig. 25), and Lydd,[3] but the general absence of all reference to aisles in the surviving descriptions quoted above has a significance which is accented by the direct statement in connexion with Ely that Leofwin built the south aisle and joined it to the rest of the building; presumably he pierced an arcade in a previously aisleless church wall. This conclusion is reinforced by the lack of aisles in the great majority of secondary churches which survive, such

[1] *Roy. Com. on Hist. Mons. (England), Bucks.,* ii, p. 332.
[2] *Ibid., Hunts.,* p. 199.
[3] *Arch. Cantiana,* xxxvii, p. 177.

as Breamore,[1] St. Mary, Dover,[2] Worth,[3] and Hadstock.[4] The subsidiary altars in the larger churches were still accommodated, as they were normally in the previous age, in the porticus communicating with the main building only by doorways. Remains of several of these porticus survive at Deerhurst and elsewhere, and their form must now be considered, as it had an important bearing on the evolution

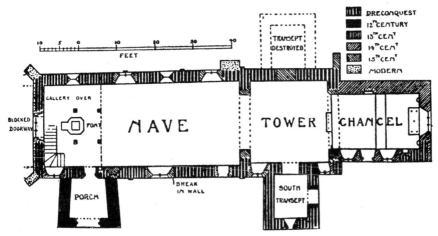

Fig. 26. Breamore, Hants.

of the English type of the cruciform plan. We have seen, in an earlier chapter, how one pair of porticus of the seventh-century churches was normally placed, symmetrically, flanking the east end of the nave. The next step was the formation of a crossing, or rather of a space between the nave and the chancel; this feature first makes its appearance at Brixworth, but the porticus, which presumably attended it, have been destroyed. When next it appears, in the tenth century, the plan has become stereotyped; the Brixworth 'crossing' is retained and the attendant porticus have assumed the form of small transepts; they are, however,

[1] Baldwin Brown, *op. cit.* (Architecture), 2nd edit., p. 349.
[2] *Ibid.*, p. 352, and *Arch. Cantiana*, v, p. 1.
[3] Baldwin Brown, *op. cit.*, p. 363, and *Arch. Journ.*, xiii, p. 196.
[4] *Roy. Com. on Hist. Mons.* (England), Essex, i, p. 144.

much narrower than the 'crossing' which forms two salient angles between the chancel and the transepts. In the earlier examples the transeptal chapels are entered only by doorways as at Deerhurst, and the size of these openings is some indication of the stage in evolution and presumably also in date attained by each individual example; thus Breamore (Fig. 26) has rather larger openings than Deerhurst. Repton [1] (before the transept was enlarged to the west) appears to have had a single narrow arch on each side, whilst at Hadstock (Fig. 27 and Pl. 44) the arches were relatively broad. At St. Mary, Dover (Fig. 28), both arches have been replaced by later work. The last stage in development appears to have been the widening of the transeptal chapels to the full width of the crossing, and this was exemplified at Great Paxton (Fig. 25). An offshoot from this type is to be found at Worth (Pl. 35), where the plan (Fig. 29) is varied by the absence of the west wall of the 'crossing', thus making it continuous with the nave. Something of the same sort is exemplified on a small scale in the little chapel of Bradford-on-Avon[2] (Pl. 37), and perhaps at Bishopstone [3] (Sussex). In both of these churches, however, the chapels are placed farther west and partake also of the nature of porches. One other feature may be noticed in this place—the commonly lofty proportions of Anglo-Saxon buildings as compared to their width. This appears to have been due to a desire to raise the unglazed windows above the level of the heads of those within; it was copied in Anglo-Scottish buildings, such as St. Rule's, St. Andrews, after the Conquest.

Before leaving the subject of the general characteristics of tenth- and eleventh-century English churches, something must be said of the types exemplified by the small village churches which form the great mass of the surviving

[1] Baldwin Brown, *op. cit.*, p. 313.
[2] *Ibid.*, p. 296.
[3] *Antiquary*, N.S., viii (1911), and *Sussex Arch. Colls.*, ii.

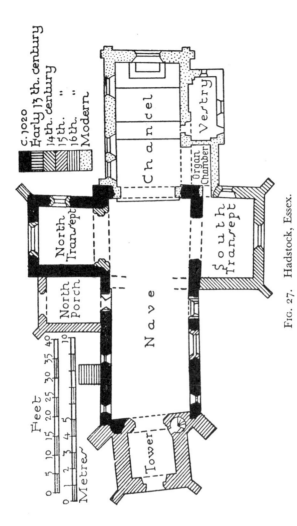

Fig. 27. Hadstock, Essex.

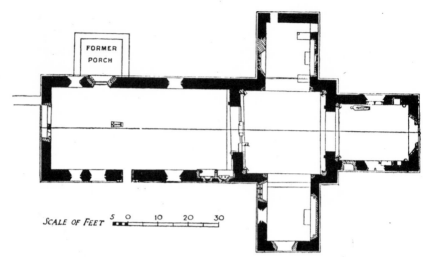

SCALE OF FEET

FIG. 28. Dover, St. Mary in Castro.

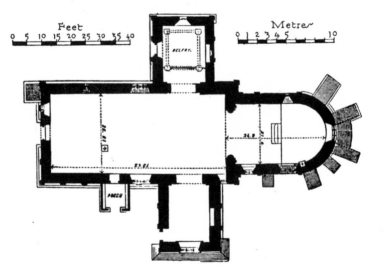

Feet

Metres

FIG. 29. Worth, Sussex (before restoration).

examples of pre-Conquest architecture. By far the commonest type is that consisting only of a rectangular chancel
and nave of the same form. The chancel usually approxi-
mates to a square, and the nave to rather less than two

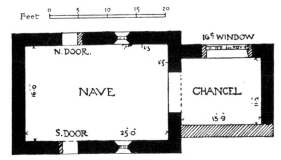

FIG. 30. Odda's Chapel, Deerhurst.

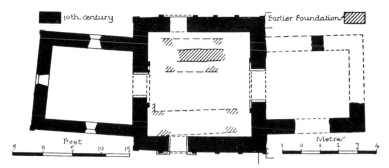

FIG. 31. Barton-on-Humber.

squares. Their distinguishing features are a common absence
of care in setting out—the angles are seldom right angles—
and the extreme narrowness of the chancel-arch. Good
examples of this simple type are to be found at Chickney
(Fig. 34), Inworth, and Strethall in Essex,[1] at Wareham,
Dorset (Fig. 36), and at Kirkdale [2] (Fig. 32) in Yorkshire;
the latest is of importance as being dated by an inscription
to about the year 1060. The addition of a tower is the
most common variant. Normally they occur at the west

[1] Plans of Chickney and Strethall in *Roy. Com. on Hist. Mons. (England), Essex,*
i, pp. 62 and 296; of Inworth in *ibid.,* iii, p. 139.
[2] *V.C.H. Yorks., N. Riding,* i, p. 521.

end of the building as at Barnack [1] (Northants.), Holy
Trinity, Colchester,[2] St. Benet, Cambridge [3] (Pl. 52), and
St. Michael, Oxford,[4] but sometimes between the chancel
and nave, as at Langford [5] (Oxon.) (Pl. 52) and probably
at Guildford, St. Mary.[6]

Two other types deserve a short mention. The first is

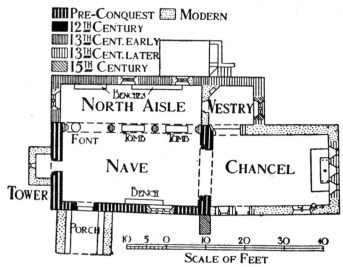

FIG. 32.   Kirkdale, Yorks.

the curious form of plan in which the tower forms the body
of the church, with a small chancel projecting towards the
east. The best example is the church of Barton-on-Humber [7] (Fig. 31), where there is a small annexe also to the
west of the tower. A similar plan has been suggested at
Earls Barton [8] (Pl. 39) (Northants.) and Broughton (Lincs.).
The type survived the Conquest, and is probably exemplified in the twelfth-century church at Fingest [9] (Bucks.).

[1] Baldwin Brown, *op. cit.*, p. 277.   [2] *Roy. Com. on Hist. Mons., Essex,* iii, p. 34.
[3] *Camb. Ant. Soc. Comm.,* xxviii, p. 83.
[4] Baldwin Brown, *op. cit.*, p. 474.
[5] H. Paintin, *Three Oxfordshire Churches* (Kencot, Broadwell, and Langford),
1911.
[6] *V.C.H. Surrey,* iii, p. 564.   [7] Baldwin Brown, *op. cit.*, p. 291.
[8] Baldwin Brown, *op. cit.*, p. 284.
[9] *Roy. Com. on Hist. Mons., Bucks. South,* p. 157.

The second type is of a more doubtful character; its distinguishing feature is the presence of a large vestibule forming a westward extension of the nave. There is or was

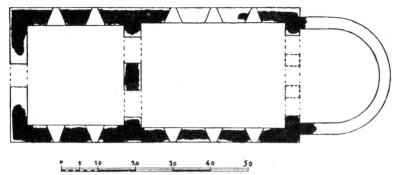

FIG. 33. South Elmham, Suffolk.

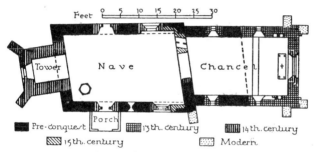

FIG. 34. Chickney, Essex.

evidence of this division at Boarhunt [1] (Hants), but the most remarkable example is at the 'Old Minster' (Fig. 33), South Elmham [2] (Suffolk). Professor Baldwin Brown inclines to place this building after the Conquest, but it stands equally isolated whether it be placed then, in the tenth century, or in the seventh, as other authorities have determined. Its most curious features are the two wide openings between the nave and the vestibule, and the sleeper wall running across the broad but ruined opening between the nave and the apse. It is possible that these vestibules

[1] Baldwin Brown, *op. cit.*, p. 309.
[2] *Arch. Journ.*, lviii, p. 424, and Baldwin Brown, *op. cit.*, p. 311.

represent the western galleries for altars we have considered above; but it seems at any rate possible that the example at South Elmham supported a tower like that at North Elmham.

Of the timber churches of the late Saxon period little need be said. Only one example, built of split oak logs, survives at Greenstead [1] in Essex, but there is documentary evidence [2] that in the non-stone districts of England they were not infrequent at the time of the Conquest. They have in any case little or no bearing on the history of English ecclesiastical architecture.

In the foregoing sketch of the main features of late Saxon church-building the date of nearly all the examples cited has been assumed. Not only is there a dearth of dated buildings within the period, but the documentary evidence deals almost entirely with buildings which have disappeared. Within the limits of the period, however, it is possible to place, with assurance, not only the buildings referred to in the argument, but a large number more, of less importance, which have been examined and listed by Professor Baldwin Brown. The basis for this classification is the architectural detail employed, which is not only distinctive in itself, but is, in many cases, entirely absent from the datable examples of the preceding and succeeding ages. It is thus only within certain limits that any real uncertainty exists as to the date of a late Saxon church with distinctive features; within these limits one can only assume a development, progressive in some particulars, retrograde perhaps in others, and arrange one's examples in such a sequence as commends itself either on the grounds of general probability or individual theory. These important architectural details will be considered in the next chapter.

[1] *Roy. Com. on Hist. Mons., Essex*, ii, p. 112.
[2] E.g. at St. Pancras, Lewes. See list in Dietrichson, *Norske Stavkirker.*

PLATE 35

WORTH, SUSSEX, APSE AND CHURCH
FROM SE.
10th century

WING, BUCKS., APSE
10th century

PLATE 36

DOVER, ST. MARY IN CASTRO, DURING RESTORATION
late 10th or early 11th century

BREAMORE, HANTS, FROM THE SE.
mid 10th century

Chapter V

CONSTRUCTIONAL AND ARCHITECTURAL
DETAILS

(a) Walling

ANGLO-SAXON constructional detail of the Carolingian age cannot be said to emulate the form and variety of facing which is exemplified in continental work of the same period. The brick cordons, the regular bands of herring-bone work, the diamond-setting of the facing-stones and other decorative features which the continental builders inherited from the Roman builders in Gaul, are hardly exemplified in existing examples of English work;[1] and it is only with the Norman influx under Edward the Confessor that some few of them, adopted by the Normans, seem to have made a belated appearance in this country.

Later Anglo-Saxon walling is commonly of rubble, very roughly, if at all, coursed, and homogeneous throughout the wall, which is commonly between $2\frac{1}{2}$ and 3 ft. in thickness. This thickness is seldom exceeded even in the major churches, and forms a very distinctive feature of pre-Conquest work, as the Norman builders seldom employed walling of less than 3 ft. in thickness, even in their smallest buildings. Occasionally the materials of the wall are set herring-bone fashion, in courses, as can be seen sporadically throughout Deerhurst church, in the apse of Stanley St. Leonard,[2] at Stoke d'Abernon,[3] and elsewhere, but this method is so uncommon in definitely pre-Conquest building, and so common in building of the succeeding age, that it may normally be taken as an indication of post-Conquest date.

[1] The small chancel of the ruined church of Stone by Ospringe (Kent) has brick bands and some attempt at a polychrome decoration of the wall-surface, by the alternating use of different materials.
[2] *Archaeologia*, lxxi, p. 222.   [3] Baldwin Brown, *op. cit.*, p. 480.

Anglo-Saxon ashlar is uncommon and without distinctive character; the best example is the little church of St. Laurence, Bradford-on-Avon (Pl. 37). Here it is well coursed and, comparatively, a good piece of masonry.

The quoins at the angles of a building are sometimes entirely lacking in this period, particularly in the 'non-stone' counties of the east and south-east coast, the rubble materials of the wall (commonly flint) forming also its angles. This is indeed, in this district, no bad indication of pre-Conquest date, as it but rarely occurs in the succeeding period. When quoins are employed, they also supply valuable evidence of date if they belong to one or other of two types. These types may be termed the 'Megalithic' and the 'long and short', both of them being largely confined to the pre-Conquest period.

The megalithic quoins consist of large stones, worked on two faces only, and commonly set with their broad faces alternately on one side or other of the angle. The result has a superficial resemblance to 'long and short' work, from which it is, in reality, quite distinct. Good examples of this form of quoin are to be found at Kilpeck (Herefordshire), St. Mildred, Canterbury (Pl. 38), &c.

In 'long and short' work the stones are set upright and flat alternately in a more or less regular manner so as to form a distinctive decorative feature, the appearance being symmetrical on the two faces of the angle. Good examples occur at Wittering (Northants.), Rockland (Norfolk), and St. Benet, Cambridge (Pl. 52).

The purely decorative features in the walling of this period are of two varieties—the pilaster-strip and blind-arcading, both confined to the larger churches which have survived, and the former unrepresented in later work where its place is taken by the pilaster-buttress.

The pilaster-strip is derived directly by Professor Baldwin Brown from the *lisenen* of the Carolingian Rhineland churches, and ultimately from the ornamental pilasters with

PLATE 37

BRADFORD-ON-AVON, WILTS., SAXON CHAPEL, FROM THE NW.
early 10*th century*

PLATE 38

BARNACK, NORTHANTS., SLAB ON
S. FACE OF TOWER
10th century

CANTERBURY, ST. MILDRED,
MEGALITHIC QUOIN-STONES
10th century

PLATE 39

EARLS BARTON, NORTHANTS., W. TOWER
10th century

PLATE 40

EARLS BARTON, NORTHANTS., PILASTER-STRIPS AND ARCADING
ON S. FACE OF TOWER

10th century

caps and bases of late Roman work.[1] This derivation seems fully established, and the fact that the *lisenen* make little or no appearance in the French portion of the Carolingian Empire is significant for the immediate source from which the English Carolingian style was derived.

The English pilaster-strip in its simplest form is used to divide a wall into bays, much as is done by a buttress, but the pilaster-strip has no structural significance, its breadth and projection being both inconsiderable. In this manner it is used at Repton (Derby), Stanton Lacy (Salop), Breamore (Hants), Colne Rogers (Gloucester), and a considerable number of other places. The strips normally stand on square base-blocks, and sometimes terminate, as at Langford (Oxon.), in stepped head-blocks.[2] In occasional instances, most commonly in towers, the pilaster-strip is more generously employed, and forms a network of stone panelling on the face of the wall; this is best exemplified on the tower at Earls Barton (Northants.) (Pls. 39, 40) and occurs in a simpler form at Barton-on-Humber (Pl. 41). At the former of these places there can be little doubt that the builders, while employing traditional methods, were consciously imitating timber construction.

The more elaborate employment of pilaster-strips is often found in conjunction with a simple form of arcading; thus at Earls Barton there are two ranges of arcading, one round-headed and the other triangular; at Barton-on-Humber, too, both forms occur. At both places the arcading is formed of projecting stone strips precisely similar to the pilasters. Of the two forms the triangular is the more distinctive, and as it does not occur, or only in a very different form, in the succeeding period, it forms a valuable evidence

[1] As Rivoira points out the German *lisenen* were a direct borrowing from Italy, where the *lesena* can be traced back to Roman times. Rivoira, *Lombardic Architecture*, ii, p. 169.

[2] At Bibury (Gloucestershire) a pilaster-strip on the north side of the chancel has elaborate geometrical decoration. See illustration in *Bristol and Glos. Arch. Soc. Trans.* xli (1919), p. 188 and Fig. 49.

of date. The use of the same form for another type of arcading is exemplified at Wing (Bucks.) and Deerhurst, where
it appears in the upper part of the chancel walls as a series
of high-pitched pediments on the wall-face. In both these
types the feature is not true wall-arcading, for it supports
nothing, the forms being simply traced in stone on the wall-
surface with a very slight projection. Arcading which is
really recessed in the wall occurs at Dunham Magna (Norfolk) and at Bradford-on-Avon (St. Laurence), where it is
continued at intervals round the church, and, though of
simple form, is architectural in its composition. The round
arches spring from flat pilasters that have both capitals and
bases, and here the pilaster-strips which occur below the
arcading partake more of the nature of buttresses than in
most other examples.

The true buttress was but little used at this period; but
that it was not unknown is proved by the definite examples
found at St. Augustine's, Canterbury (Fig. 49). The
northern enlargement of St. Gregory's porticus here must
have been built some time between the middle of the
eighth century and the Conquest,[1] and, though quite a
small building, is provided with buttresses of a proportion
and projection which did not become usual before the
thirteenth century. The added vestibule of the same
church had also buttresses of deep projection at the western
angles. Abbot Wulfric's rotunda, built in the middle of the
eleventh century, is provided with flat pilaster buttresses,
placed, somewhat inconsequentially, in the middle of the
sides and not at the angles of the building. In spite of this
abundance of examples at one place it would be difficult to
cite any other instances from the surviving churches of the
ninth, tenth, and early eleventh centuries. Before leaving
the subject, some reference must be made to the remarkable

[1]. The enlargement cannot have been built until after the burial of Archbishop
Brihtwald (d. 731), whose tomb was in the main church owing to lack of space
in the original porticus. The terminal date is determined by the fact that the
buttresses of the extension underlie the south walk of the early Norman cloister.

PLATE 41

BARTON-ON-HUMBER, LINCS., TOWER, S. FACE
10th century

PLATE 42

STRETHALL, ESSEX, CHANCEL-ARCH
early 11th century

BOSHAM, SUSSEX, CHANCEL-ARCH
early to mid 11th century

semi-cylindrical shafts at the Cathedral of North Elmham (Fig. 22). These shafts, which are placed in the re-entrant angles of the transept and its flanking towers, and also round the apse, are built of the same material (pudding-stone) as, and course with, the adjoining walls; they nowhere stand to a sufficient height to show how they were finished, but enough remains of the apse to indicate that they were spaced close together round this part of the building, and most probably supported an arcade under the eaves, after the manner of numerous early Romanesque churches of Italy. They have not so far been paralleled elsewhere in England.

(b) Arches and Doorways

These two features may be taken together, as late Saxon doorways are very seldom provided with a door-check or rebate, and are thus distinguishable from archways only by their smaller size. All pre-Conquest arches of any size are semicircular, and it is only in doorways or smaller openings that the triangular head appears. The width of the chancel or transept arch varies greatly, and we have seen that in the case of the transept it may form some indication of the stage of evolution arrived at by the individual example. The same test cannot, however, be applied to the chancel arch, which varies considerably in examples which cannot be widely separated chronologically. A number of churches in the midlands and the south have chancel arches almost the full width of the eastern arm; and of these the most notable are Bosham (Sussex) (Pl. 42), Worth (Sussex) (Pl. 43), Great Paxton (Hunts.), and Wittering (Northants.) (Pl. 45). As all four are buildings of some importance, and Bosham was a 'Minster', one may perhaps surmise that the wide chancel arch was considered appropriate in a building served by a body of clergy, while the narrow arch was used in the small village or parish churches where the establishment was of one priest only. Examples of this latter form, hardly wider than a doorway, may be seen at Bradford-on-Avon, Strethall (Essex) (Pl. 42), &c.

Another feature which indicates a lack of constructive ability, and consequently an early date, is the setting back of the reveal of the arch beyond the face of the respond. This practice is commoner in the north than the south, and is not confined to pre-Conquest buildings; it was adopted to provide a broad seating for the timber centering while the arch was being built. This offset is generally found in arches of the simplest character, but the same reason is responsible for the omission, in a number of instances, of the inner order of an arch, for which an inner order of the responds appears to have been provided; this is well seen at Broughton (Lincs.).

Both arches and doorways are commonly provided, in this period, with a stone framework (Pls. 45, 46), on one face only, forming a rude sort of architrave. The stone framing is of identical form and character with the pilaster-strips of the external walls; it is commonly broken by a horizontal strip at the impost level, but above this it continues round the arch. The earliest example in England appears to be the side arches at Britford, which, as we have seen, can reasonably be dated to about 800. For the rest of our period it becomes perhaps the most common and typical of all Anglo-Saxon features and is exemplified in nearly every church of any importance.

Arch-responds, when not of the simplest rectangular form, are often provided, especially in the chancel arch, with three attached shafts. These shafts in the more usual, and perhaps earlier, form project from the outer and inner faces and from the reveal, so that the plan of the respond is symmetrical; responds of this type are to be found at Worth, Bosham (Pl. 47), Clayton (Sussex), and Wittering. In a later type, showing Norman influence, the side shafts are recessed in the wall as at Hadstock (Pl. 44) and Kirkdale, the latter definitely dated (by its inscribed sundial)

PLATE 43

N. transept arch

WORTH, SUSSEX
late 10th century

Chancel-arch

PLATE 44

HADSTOCK, ESSEX,
S. TRANSEPT RESPOND
early to mid 11th century

GT. PAXTON, HUNTS., NW.
RESPOND OF CROSSING
mid 11th century

to the reign of Edward the Confessor. A more elaborate form of respond with a multiplication of shafts is found at Great Paxton (Pl. 44).

Of continuous aisle-arcades we have very few examples, and these of a very varied nature. At Wing [1] and Lydd [2] (Kent) the piers are plain rectangular masses of masonry supporting equally plain semicircular arches with simple imposts at the springing-level. At Great Paxton [3] the piers (Pl. 46) are compound, consisting of a rectangular core, set diagonally, with an attached shaft on each face. At Ickleton (Cambs.), which though certainly post-Conquest has early features, four of the monolithic cylindrical piers are presumably re-used Roman shafts from a neighbouring villa or from Great Chesterton.[4] Both here and at Great Paxton the round arches are of simple rectangular section.

The triangular-headed doorway or opening is also a feature of the period; it is copied from the common use of the triangular form in Carolingian decoration on the Continent. The best surviving doorways of this type are at Holy Trinity, Colchester (Pl. 48), Dunham Magna, and Barton-on-Humber (Pl. 48).

Windows.

The 'double-splay' window (Pl. 49) forms one of the commonest and most distinctive features of late Anglo-Saxon architecture. As it is entirely absent from buildings of the pre-Danish period it may be looked upon as the hall-mark of the later or 'Carolingian' period. The use of the opening with an equal splay both within and without has been noticed in the Roman period,[5] and such windows also occur

[1] *Roy. Com. on Hist. Mons., Bucks. N.*, p. 331.
[2] *Arch. Cantiana*, xxxvii; 'Notes on the Churches of Romney Marsh', by F. C. Elliston Erwood.
[3] *Roy. Com. on Hist. Mons., Hunts.*, p. 198.
[4] Baldwin Brown, *op. cit.* (Architecture), 2nd ed., p. 418.
[5] E.g. the Villa of Sette Bassi. G. T. Rivoira, *Roman Architecture* (1925), p. 152. They occur also in the church of Bagnacavallo, assigned by Rivoira to the sixth century, and in later churches in Italy.

in buildings of undoubted Norman date,[1] but in both these cases the adoption of this form has been actuated by the excessive thickness of the wall in which the opening occurs, and there is, I believe, hardly an instance in England, outside our period, of a 'double-splay' window in a wall of normal dimensions. In the late Saxon period its use is almost universal, occurring with equal frequency wherever structures of this age are found and deriving, in all probability, from the Rhineland where it is also of fairly frequent occurrence. Its presence in churches such as Bradford-on-Avon and Lydd is almost conclusive evidence of the late Saxon date of these structures, which might otherwise be difficult to place. It is, furthermore, present in the chapel at Deerhurst, definitely dated to 1056. In a few instances, where the window has been long blocked, traces have been found of the wooden board with which the opening itself has been filled. These boards were built into the masonry of the opening at its narrowest point (i.e. in the middle of the wall) and were presumably pierced by a series of openings geometrically arranged, like the pierced marble slabs (*transennae*) which served a similar purpose in Italy and the east. Just such slabs, of stone, actually survive in three of the tower-windows at Barnack, where the piercings take the form of an interlaced design, and remains of a single example in wood are still to be seen at Birstall (Leicestershire). Practically all the windows of this age are round-headed with a very occasional triangular-head in tower-openings. Another fairly common form of window is the complete round, frequently used, as we have seen, in continental Carolingian buildings. In England it occurs in the clearstory of Avebury (Wilts.), at Bosham, Bibury, and Barton-on-Humber, and in the towers of Dunham Magna, St. Benet, Cambridge (Pl. 52), &c.

In general, windows of this period are of a single light only, but occasionally, as at Worth and Wing, two-light

[1] E.g. Lewes Priory (frater), Lydford Castle (keep), &c.

PLATE 45

WITTERING, NORTHANTS., CHANCEL-ARCH

10th century

CAMBRIDGE, ST. BENET, TOWER-ARCH

10th century

PLATE 46

GT. PAXTON, HUNTS., S. ARCADE
OF NAVE

mid 11th century

EARLS BARTON, NORTHANTS.,
W. DOORWAY OF TOWER

10th century

windows are introduced. The lights at Worth are divided
by a shaft, and there is no apparent provision for closing
the opening. Both the jambs and the shaft are provided
with bases and imposts, the shaft being placed near the
middle of the wall with an oblong impost-stone carried
through the wall and forming a cantilever support for the
two arches. This is the principle of the mid-wall shaft, the
origin of which must now be considered. One of the distinctive features of early Byzantine architecture, when it
began to part company from Roman tradition, was the
adoption of the super-abacus or dosseret, a block with faces
sloping outwards, inserted between the capital of a column
and the springing of the arches which it supported to in-
crease the area on which such arches might rest. This is
essentially the office performed by the cantilever capital of
the mid-wall shaft, except that the projection is emphasized
across the supported arches and suppressed on the other
two faces. This application of an early Byzantine feature
to window-openings does not seem to have been adopted in
Italy before the close of the ninth century, and is there
almost confined to the belfry openings of campanili, to
which it is eminently suited. Germany, particularly the
Rhineland, copied it at a rather later date, and it seems
improbable that it can have reached this country much
before the end of the tenth century. In England it is represented by two forms, the more primitive a flat oblong
stone laid flat on the top of the mid-wall shaft, as at
Worth (nave) (Pl. 50), Barton-on-Humber (tower), and
Brixworth (tower), and the second and more advanced type
(represented in Italy and Germany) of an oblong capital
deeply corbelled in two directions, as at Sompting (tower)
and Jarrow (tower). It is instructive, from the point of
view of the Carolingian parentage of late Anglo-Saxon
architecture, to note the quite different method employed
in Normandy, and northern France generally, to meet the
same problem. Here, normally, the double-headed open-

ing is set in an arched recess sufficiently deep to permit of the springing of the two heads from the abacus of the central shaft.

The form of shaft most commonly used in England is the well-known baluster type. This appears as early as the end of the seventh century in the porch at Monkwearmouth (Pl. 6), still *in situ*, and in other examples preserved in that church and at Jarrow. These early balusters, however, are quite distinctive in character; they are turned on a lathe and depart but little from the cylindrical form, the mouldings being not much more than grooves and bands cut on the surface. The late Saxon balusters (Pl. 50), on the other hand, generally exhibit a marked bulge, too gross to be termed entasis, and are ringed with numerous mouldings, not always symmetrical, but generally disposed to form a cap, a base, and a band.

Towers

The origin of bell-towers is a subject which has a crucial bearing on the dating of pre-Conquest architecture, and must thus be considered in some detail. The most diverse views have been held on the subject by continental archaeologists, and the controversy cannot yet be said to be finally settled. Lasteyrie [1] and Enlart [2] have both maintained that church-towers existed from the sixth century onwards, and cite in favour of this view the descriptions, given by Gregory of Tours and Fortunatus, of the tower-like erections over the crossing of the transept, which inspired the later Carolingian builders. They also argue from the mosaic at S. Maria Maggiore, Rome, and the carvings on the doors of S. Sabina in the same city, that towers were in use in Italy at an equally early date. It is not, however, suggested that any of these were bell-towers; the French examples,

---

[1] R. de Lasteyrie, *L'architecture religieuse en France à l'époque romane*, chap. xii.
[2] C. Enlart, 'Manuel d'archéologie française', *Architecture religieuse*, i, 3rd ed., p. 137.

being mainly of timber, were obviously unsuited to this purpose, and the Italian pictorial examples, if indeed they may rank as evidence at all, seem more closely allied to the staircase towers of certain Syrian churches than to the later bell-tower. The French authorities cite also literary evidence of a bell-tower at S. Martin, Tours (its inscription was copied on a bell-tower at the Vatican by Stephen II, 752–7), and another at Fontenelle, mentioned in the chronicle of that abbey as built *c*. 734–8. Unfortunately the form of these towers is indeterminate; the word applied to that at Fontenelle (*turricula*) might imply anything from a bell-cote upwards.

We are thus thrown back on the definite evidence of surviving examples of bell-towers, in the later sense of the term, to arrive at any conclusion as to the age of this form of structure. It is quite certain that no surviving bell-tower in France can be dated before the tenth century and probably not before the second half of that century, but it has been commonly asserted that in Italy numerous examples have survived of a far earlier date. Corrado Ricci has, however, recently asserted,[1] categorically, that no Italian bell-tower was erected before the second half of the ninth century. His main arguments are briefly as follows: (1) that Italian campanili are erected haphazard in any available position, thus dissociating them from any original connexion with the plan of the church, original parts of which are sometimes destroyed or mutilated by their erection; (2) that the materials of the earliest examples include re-used material of the seventh, eighth, and ninth centuries; (3) that the Liber Pontificalis of the Ravenna churches, dating from the first half of the ninth century and describing the buildings in detail, makes no mention of a bell-tower at any one of them.

The conclusion seems inevitable that the bell-tower, as we understand it, was not introduced until the ninth

[1] C. Ricci, *Romanesque Architecture in Italy* (1925).

century in Italy; and it need not, perhaps, be looked for in England before the tenth century. This is entirely in accord with the evidence presented by the pre-Conquest remains of this country. Neither of the early groups of churches has any trace of such an appendage, and all the surviving examples bear internal evidence of their late date.

Three of these towers (Monkwearmouth, Brixworth, and Corbridge) actually stand on the structure of west porches of the early period, and the same was perhaps also the case at Bradwell-on-Sea, but both tower and porch have now been destroyed.

The external form of these tenth- and early eleventh-century towers presents two different types which apparently existed side by side. The more individualistic of these is the type of tower (Pl. 51) which rises from ground to parapet, or at any rate to the belfry, without horizontal division or offset to mark the stages, and in which the impression of height is sometimes enhanced by a slight batter in the surfaces of two or all of the walls. Perhaps the earliest example of this type of tower is that at Deerhurst[1] (Pl. 33), but it continued throughout the period and overlapped the Norman Conquest, being represented by two or more examples[2] in the Yorkshire Wolds definitely dated by Mr. J. Bilson to the early years of the twelfth century. These, however, are evidence of an unusually late survival of Saxon tradition, and do not invalidate the claim of this type of tower to be a distinctively Saxon feature. The other and more ornate type of tower (Pls. 39, 41, 51) is best represented in the stone-producing counties of Northampton and Lincoln. The stages are divided up in the usual way and the openings are at once more numerous and more ornate.[3]

[1] Other examples exist at Corbridge, Oxford (St. Michael), Clapham (Beds.) (Pl. 51), St. Peter at Gowts, and other Lincolnshire churches.
[2] Weaverthorpe and Wharram-le-Street; see *Archaeologia*, lxxii, p. 51, and lxxiii, p. 55.
[3] E.g. Barnack (Pl. 51), Earls Barton (Pl. 39), Barton-on-Humber (Pl. 41), &c.

PLATE 47

SOMPTING, SUSSEX, RESPOND OF
TOWER-ARCH
early 11th century

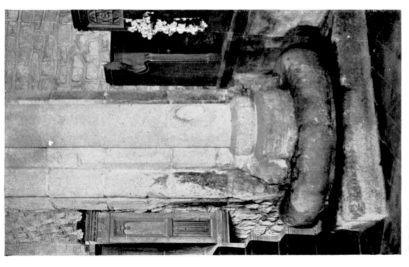

BOSHAM, SUSSEX, RESPOND-BASE
OF CHANCEL-ARCH
early to mid 11th century

PLATE 48

BARTON-ON-HUMBER, LINCS., N. DOORWAY
OF TOWER
10th century

COLCHESTER, HOLY TRINITY, W. DOORWAY
OF TOWER
late 10th or early 11th century

An unusual feature of some of the Saxon towers is the evidence they retain of their use for domestic purposes, or at any rate for purposes not immediately connected with the ritual of the church. This is particularly the case with the tower at Deerhurst; a building of curious oblong plan, with the two lower stories divided into two chambers by a partition wall. All the upper stories of the tower must have been approached by wooden staircases or ladders either within or without the building, and all the eastern rooms have some communication either by a door or a window with the church. No satisfactory explanation of the purpose of these chambers has yet been put forward; Deerhurst was a monastic church, but there is no reason to suppose that it was unprovided in the tenth century with the usual monastic buildings grouped round a cloister, for by this time the normal monastic plan had been generally adopted. It should, however, be remembered that the occasional use of the towers of churches, and even the upper stories of aisles, for domestic purposes, lingered on far into the Middle Ages, especially in Ireland and Scotland,[1] though to what officer of the convent the use of such rooms was assigned seems uniformly unrecorded. The most remarkable feature of these towers, however, is the presence, in a number of them, of doorways on the external faces, high above the ground. It is usual to explain these doorways by the postulation of timber or masonry annexes against the north, south, or west faces of the tower as the case may be. This may satisfactorily account for a number of instances, but there are others, such as at Earls Barton, where the height above the ground and the elaborate decoration of the wall-surface of the tower seem to negative the possibility of the existence of such an annexe in the original design. It seems more reasonable to suppose that, in, at any rate, the smaller churches, where this feature occurs it was provided for occasional access to the upper

[1] E.g. at Leiston Abbey, Suffolk; Torphichen; Holy Cross Abbey, Thurles, &c.

stages by means of a ladder, when repairs had to be done; it being thought undesirable to cumber the ground stage (which was commonly used as a porch) with a permanent staircase.[1] In the few instances where a pre-Conquest tower is provided with a masonry staircase, as at Brixworth, Brigstock, and perhaps Great Hale, these external openings do not occur. In the larger churches the former existence of annexes at the west end of the building is highly probable, and is illustrated by the documentary description of the church at Winchester already quoted, and by the actual remains of the walls on the three external faces of the tower at Netheravon (Wilts.), though the presence of the rebated jambs of the north and south doorways indicates a post-Conquest date.

Before leaving the subject of towers attention must be called to the example at Sompting (Sussex) which alone of its fellows has retained its original capping (Pl. 53). This consists of a high-pitched gable on each face, from which rise the ridges of the pyramidal roof, the faces of which are continued down over the spaces between the gables. This was a common form of roof in the Rhineland,[2] but whether or not it was the normal method of covering a small Saxon tower we do not know; the presence of certain decorative detail (p. 135) indicates that it should be assigned to the first half of the eleventh century.

Porches

Late Anglo-Saxon porches, where they occur, are commonly on a larger scale than seems at all necessary for their primary purpose. That they are essentially the successors of the porticus of the earlier plan can hardly be doubted, and from these they differ little except in the presence of the

---

[1] The occasional use of this feature for defensive purposes, as in the round towers of Ireland, must not be overlooked. At Wickham church, Berkshire, the Saxon west tower seems only to have been approached by a doorway, some 8 ft. above the ground, in the south wall. See *V.C.H., Berks.*, iv, p. 124.

[2] E.g. Laach; Liége; St. Bartholomew; Cologne, Holy Apostles; &c.

PLATE 49

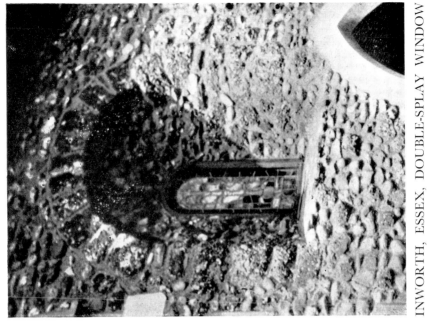

INWORTH, ESSEX, DOUBLE-SPLAY WINDOW
10th or early 11th century

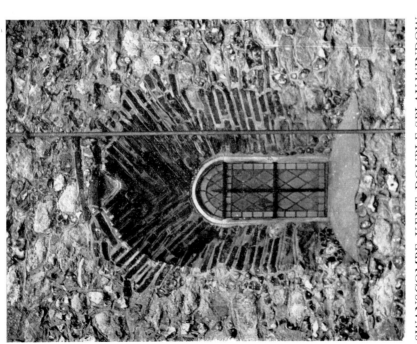

SWANSCOMBE, KENT, DOUBLE-SPLAY WINDOW
10th or early 11th century

PLATE 50

a. WORTH, SUSSEX, WINDOW IN N. WALL OF NAVE
late 10th century

b. DOVER, ST. MARY IN CASTRO, BALUSTER-SHAFTS
10th century

outer doorway. It is the doorway which gives the key to
their secondary use, for in the majority of cases either it

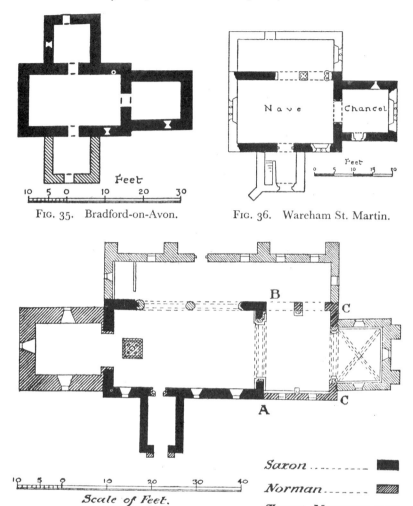

FIG. 35.   Bradford-on-Avon.   FIG. 36.   Wareham St. Martin.

Saxon ....

Norman ....

Trans-Norman-
Early English..

Scale of Feet.

FIG. 37.   Bishopstone, Sussex.

or the inner doorway is placed noticeably to the west of the
axial line of the porch. This may be seen in the north
porch at Bradford-on-Avon and in the south porch at
Bishopstone. The only object that this arrangement could

have served is the placing of an altar against the east wall,
thus making the structure serve the dual purpose of a
porch and a chapel. That this was indeed the case is
further evidenced by the description of the Saxon cathedral
of Canterbury, where the base of the south tower served
both as a porch and as a chapel of St. Gregory.

Mouldings

Late Anglo-Saxon mouldings, it must be admitted, are
marked by a poverty of ideas and an entire lack of appreciation of form, which is only emphasized in the few instances
where the mason attempted any elaboration. In the early
period the only examples of any consequence which survive
are the capitals and bases of the columns of Reculver; here
the base-mould (Fig. 38) has some sense of form in that the
lower members are bolder and of greater projection than
the upper; the mouldings furthermore are enriched, but
there is no trace of that attempt to copy a classical outline
which can be discerned in the most degraded Romano-
British examples. The Reculver capital has a moulded
necking and above it a series of sloping bands each set back
from the one below, like the classical architrave. It seems
unlikely that this was the finished form, and it may be that
the capital was originally furnished with applied decoration,
perhaps in the form of metal leaves attached to bands of the
same material in the grooves of the stonework.

The later Saxon mouldings have not even the slight
sense of form of the Reculver base; they follow no apparent
course of development and give little or no indication of
date; each mason would appear to have been a law unto
himself and to have produced what seemed to him good
without regard to what his neighbour might be doing.
The result is that a collection of Saxon mouldings produces
a large variety of examples which have only in common
their general ineptitude.[1] The same features are discernible

[1] An exception should be noted, to this generalization, in the well-formed

in the drawn mouldings which occur in the numerous
architectural enrichments of Ethelwold's Benedictional and

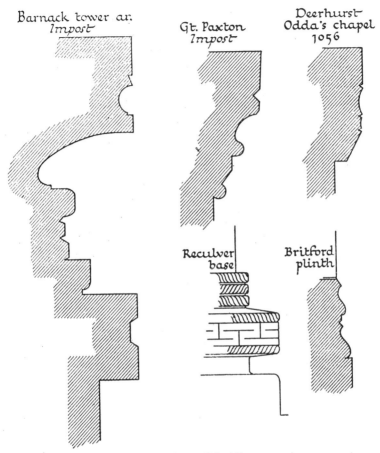

FIG. 38. Saxon Mouldings.

other manuscripts. They have this much in common, that
their acutely pointed projections and collections of insignificant members indicate the hand of the worker in
wood rather than the stone-mason, and whereas the thirteenth and fourteenth centuries carried the stone-cutter's
art into the domain of the woodworker, the reverse seems

plinth moulding of the north arch at Britford (Fig. 38), which follows closely
the lines of a modern skirting mould.

to have been the case in the pre-Conquest period. It is only in the eleventh century that some order was evolved out of this chaos, mainly by extensive borrowings from the Norman school (Fig. 38, Odda's Chapel), and the bold rolls of that province begin to make their appearance. Perhaps the most remarkable example of mouldings of the native type is that exhibited by the tower-arch at Barnack (Fig. 38); here the general effect is that of a series of thin slabs each set with a different projection but grouped into two main salients of equal depth. The result is barbaric in the extreme, and does not seem to have inspired any copyist.[1]

Some more definite conclusions can be arrived at by the study of the form of the capitals of shafts and columns, which seem to follow a more general fashion and to be groupable into two main types. These types are based on the cylinder or sphere in one case and on the cube in the other, the former being the earlier and perhaps indigenous form and the latter an introduction from the Continent. The commonest form of the cylindrical or spherical type is the bulbous capital, which makes its appearance perhaps as early as the end of the eighth and held its place well into the eleventh century. It is found, accompanied by the bulbous base, on the panels with figure-sculpture at Breedon (Leicestershire) and Castor (Northants.) assignable to c. 800, on numerous manuscripts of the same and a later date, and on the capitals at Great Paxton (Hunts.) (Pl. 46), which must date from near the middle of the eleventh century. The bulbous base survived the Conquest, and is a not uncommon feature in early Norman building in this country. Another but less common form of the cylindrical type is the conical capital, which appears in its simplest form at Wittering (Northants.) accompanied by bases of the same shape. But the most remarkable instances of this form are the conical capitals (Fig. 39) of nook-shafts, found on the

[1] The impost moulding of the reset doorway at St. John's sub Castro at Lewes is remarkable as being executed in Purbeck or Sussex marble.

Fig. 39. Capitals from St. Alkmund's, Derby.

site of St. Alkmund's, Derby,[1] but of which the present location is unknown. They are unusually tall in proportion to their diameter and, with the rest of the stone from which they are cut, are enriched with a profusion of haphazard and somewhat barbaric ornament; the angle of one stone, above the capital, is carved into a human head. The recessed or nook-shaft of these capitals seems to place them in the eleventh century.

The cubical capital seems to belong definitely to the later part of the period, though it appears, not as a separate capital but as the finish, both at the top and bottom of a baluster-shaft in Brixworth tower, probably of the tenth century. Its origin has been traced from various sources, and it appears sporadically in various places and at various times from the sixth century onwards, without there being any traceable connexion between these occasional examples. It does not seem to have appeared in Germany earlier than the tenth, and did not become the rule in Normandy much before the twelfth century. Its office is to effect the transition from the circle to the square, and its most usual form is the cushion-capital. The English examples of this form are almost all to be found in the border-line churches of Lincolnshire, and a variant produced by cutting a triangular facet from each side of the square appears in the same district about the same time. A slightly different treatment of the cubical capital is exemplified at Hadstock (Pl. 44), which may be assigned to the first half of the eleventh century.

Capitals imitated more or less remotely from classical examples are to be found at St. Augustine's, Canterbury, Sompting (Pl. 47), and elsewhere, but the consideration of these must be left to the chapter on Ornament.

---

[1] *Arch. Journ.*, ii, pp. 86–7, with illustration.

PLATE 51

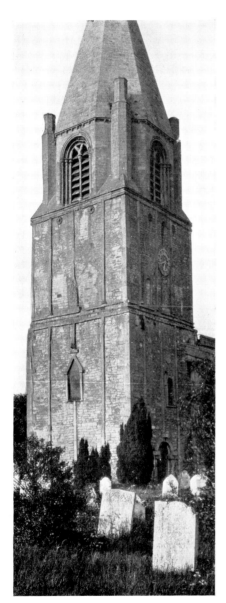

BARNACK, NORTHANTS.,
W. TOWER
mid 10th century (Belfry later)

CLAPHAM, BEDS., W. TOWER
10th century (Belfry later)

PLATE 52

CAMBRIDGE, ST. BENET, W. TOWER
10th century (except large side-windows)

LANGFORD, OXON., CENTRAL TOWER
mid 11th century

Chapter VI

DECORATION AND ORNAMENT IN THE LATE SAXON PERIOD

THE materials for the study of late Saxon ornament are largely confined, as in the previous period, to isolated monuments, cross-shafts, and the like, and carving makes but little appearance as an architectural enrichment. The great majority of examples, as before, are to be found in the northern counties, and here was produced a blend of Anglian and Scandinavian ornament which is not represented to a like degree in the midlands or the south. On the other hand the level of execution in the north shows a lamentable falling-off from the achievements of the earlier age, while the rest of England maintained a higher level, and in places reproduced the Scandinavian forms with little or no admixture of the native element.

Scandinavian artistic influence seems to have preceded, by a few years, the actual settlement of Danes or Northmen in England. It appears on a cross-shaft erected in memory of one of the abbesses of Hackness, whose succession ceased with the destruction of the monastery in 869. It is not, therefore, safe to assign all traces of this foreign style to a date at the end of the eighth century or later. There are, on the other hand, two groups of carvings which can be dated with some certainty from other than artistic grounds. The earlier of these is the collection of shafts and tomb-slabs preserved in the church at Ramsbury (Wilts.), which should, in all reasonable probability, date from after the establishment of the see there in 906 (Pl. 54). The later group is the collection of cross-shafts, &c., found in and under the chapter-house at Durham (Pl. 64 and Fig. 40), which must date between the establishment of the see there in 995 and the erection of the chapter-house about 1100–10.

FIG. 40. Durham Chapter-house, cross-heads, early eleventh century.

It is unfortunate that these two groups are at opposite ends of the kingdom; but they may serve, in any case, as indications of the type of work being produced in the north and south at their respective dates.

We have seen in Chapter III how the vine-scroll of Northumbria acclimatized itself in Mercia towards the end of the eighth century, and we find it still surviving there and in Wessex in the ninth century; in its final and most degraded form as a series of circles and rosettes it appears on a shaft at Ramsbury (Pl. 54) which no doubt belongs to the early part of the tenth century. A most important example in the series is the font at Deerhurst (Pl. 55), where two bands are carved with vine-scroll in a perfectly recognizable form; the main feature of the decoration, however, is a deep band of double spirals without the trumpet-form, which covers most of the upper part of the font. Double spirals of an almost identical type [1] occur on a pendant found in the Trewhiddle hoard, and fortunately this hoard is very closely dated, by the accompanying coins, to about the year 875. We thus get an approximate date for the Deerhurst font, and probably also for the sculptured tympanum at Castor (Northants.) which has a similar ornament round the margin. This third example is of very simple form, and the rendering of the figure which it encloses is so like that of the large figures at Breedon that we may perhaps assign it to the first half of the ninth century.

The Trewhiddle hoard, a collection of silver objects found at Trewhiddle in Cornwall in 1774 and now in the British Museum, is of great importance as giving an approximate date to a series of other metal objects bearing similar decoration. This decoration known as the Trewhiddle style is essentially English, and consists of foliage (ivy and palmette), loose interlace, and distorted beasts, set with considerable decorative sense in a framework of small

---

[1] This form of double spiral also appears in pagan Saxon art but seems to be absent in the intermediate period.

panels. These subjects are all rather different and more stylized renderings of motifs familiar in the preceding period, with the exception of the palmette. This last is best exemplified in the Wallingford Sword (Ashmolean Museum) (Pl. 56) and on a metal brooch in private possession;[1] and being a simple form, not requiring great skill to reproduce, it was adopted by the stone-carver, generally in preference to the acanthus, down to the end of the Saxon period. It can be recognized in the simple leaves of the Sompting capitals and in the decorative carving at Hadstock. The Trewhiddle style bears little trace of the Carolingian acanthus, and equally little of Scandinavian influence.

We must now turn to consider the effect of these two foreign influences on later Saxon art. The Carolingian acanthus is most in evidence in the tenth-century manuscripts of the Winchester School, which are almost overwhelmed by florid decoration of this type. In the north of England, however, it made little or no impression, for here the long Danish dominion and the strong admixture of Danish blood seem to have barred anything except Danish influence. In the south there is so little decorative stone-carving which can be dated with any certainty to this period, that the infrequent appearance of the acanthus need cause no surprise. It occurs definitely, however, on capitals found at St. Augustine's, Canterbury, on the carved panels on Barnack tower (Pl. 38), on the shaft-capitals of the tower at Langford (Oxon.), on a capital of the chancel-arch at Bibury, and, in true Carolingian form, as a border to one of the carved panels at Chichester (Pl. 62).[2] It is possible, however, that an example of the highest order survives in the great cross-shaft in the church-yard at Wolverhampton (Pl. 57). It has been usual to assign this fine and accomplished work to the twelfth cen-

[1] See *The Antiquary*, N.S. vi, p. 269. Some unnecessary doubts have been cast on its authenticity.

[2] A debased example of the same use of the acanthus as a border is to be found in the slab with a Rood (Pl. 62) at Stepney (Middlesex).

PLATE 53

SOMPTING, SUSSEX, W. TOWER
early 11th century

PLATE 54

RAMSBURY, WILTS., FRAGMENTS OF
SHAFTS
early 10th century

WEST CAMEL, SOMERSET, CROSS-SHAFT
early 10th century

tury, but in form it certainly belongs to the pre-Conquest age and its decoration combines the Carolingian acanthus with the Anglian beast. The lack of examples in stone-carving is to a certain extent made up by the survival of certain ivories, including croziers of the tau-form, which may be dated to the first half of the eleventh century.[1]

A second well-known Carolingian motif, the caulicula,[2] a species of voluted crocket, common in Italy, is represented in this country only by a panel with a carved figure of Christ at the bishop's palace at Gloucester and possibly on a capital (?) from Hexham, now at Durham.

We must now turn to the opposing and much stronger influence which dominated the north of England. The earlier history of Scandinavian ornament need not detain us, as it has no immediate bearing on our present subject. Two only of the later phases of that history may be said to directly affect the issue; these are the phases known respectively as the Jellinge and the Ringerike styles. The Jellinge style is so called from objects found in the royal burial mounds at Jellinge in Jutland. According to Professor Brøndsted, it first makes its appearance in Scandinavia about the middle of the ninth century, and makes an almost equally early appearance in the north of England. While inheriting certain elements from the earlier Scandinavian styles, it owes some of its most distinctive features to Irish originals. The animal forms in this style retain their traditional attenuated ribbon-shape, but are generally speaking well-formed and coherent beasts, distinguished by their double outline, spiral joints, backward-bent heads, and

---

[1] In the British and Victoria and Albert Museums. The tau-form of crozier survived the Norman Conquest in this country, but became increasingly uncommon. A dated example is represented on the tomb of Abbot Isarn of St. Victor, Marseilles, 1048, and another was found in the tomb of Abbot Morard of St. Germain, Paris, d. 1014. See Cahier and Martin, *Mélanges d'archéologie*, iv, 174.

[2] It makes its appearance before the Carolingian age in Italy, where the earliest dated example is the Ciborium at S. Giorgio in Valpolicella, 712; see R. Cattaneo, *Architecture in Italy*, p. 98.

nose-lappets. They are accompanied by more or less elaborate ribbon-interlace, which, however, does not begin to overpower and disintegrate the animal-forms until the style had passed its zenith, about the middle of the tenth century. Towards the close of the century a new form of animal appears, called by Brøndsted the 'Great Beast', which thenceforward fills the middle of the picture and is a more or less naturalistic presentation of an animal with proportionate limbs, and entwined with interlace which takes the form of a snake. The form of branched interlace with free binding-rings, which is also characteristic of the style, makes little show in English art and therefore need not detain us.

The interaction of this Scandinavian style on the north of England and of that of the north of England on Scandinavia is an extremely interesting and instructive study of the evolution of decorative ornament. The monuments of the north of England provide a long series of examples illustrating the prolonged attempt of the Jellinge ribbon-beast to supplant the native Anglian beast of the earlier period. This attempt was not wholly successful, for often the two forms of beast occur side by side on the same cross-shaft, the Anglian beast sometimes borrowing the double outline and spiral joints of its rival and sometimes retaining its natural form. Here and there, however, as on the slab (Fig. 41) at Levisham (Yorks.), the Jellinge beast is reproduced almost in its unaltered Scandinavian form, while the branched and angular interlace at Plumbland (Cumberland) is a very near copy of the true Jellinge type. In Northumbria the beast, whatever its form, always retained its individuality and was never disintegrated into mere ornament; this steady refusal to allow its ordinary ornamental motif to be side-tracked is exemplified on two of the cross-heads from Durham which must date from after 995 and consequently to near the close of the period.

The corresponding influence of Northumbria on Scandinavia is seen, according to Brøndsted, in the introduction there of the 'Great Beast', which is the Anglian beast with its Scandinavian modifications, transported overseas. Its appearance on the runestone of Harold Bluetooth may be dated *c.* 980.

Before turning to the second phase of Scandinavian ornament it will be convenient to consider first the other motifs on the Northumbrian cross-shafts and slabs. The interlace retains its place until the end in a much coarsened and

FIG. 41.   Levisham, Yorks., slab, tenth century.

clumsy form; the vine-scroll lingers on for some time in a degraded form but finally dies out; it is not represented in the Durham series. The best examples of work of this age, however, are to be found on the western side of the Pennines, and of these the foremost example is the well-known shaft at Gosforth (Pl. 57). The form of this shaft, round below and merging (by means of four inverted curves like the sharpening of a pencil) into a square above has been derived by Mr. Collingwood [1] from a timber original. The theory is an attractive one and would be convincing were it not for the occurrence of the round shaft with semi-classical carving at Reculver. This so evidently derives from the late Roman carved shafts, like that at Mainz, Germany, that the transition from the round to the square, observable in the midland and north-eastern shafts, so reminiscent of the squaring of timber, loses some of its significance. This particular form is nearly datable in the

[1] W. G. Collingwood, *Northumbrian Crosses of the Pre-Norman Age*, p. 5.

example known as the pillar of Eliseg [1] (Denbighshire) to early in the ninth century, which may perhaps be taken as a central date for the type.[2]

Gosforth cross is further notable as the finest example surviving in England of the 'wheel-head' cross. This form is another indication of late (i.e. ninth-century or later) date. It never occurs in England in the standing crosses of the pre-Danish series, and may well have been introduced from Ireland, where it is the standard type of the great standing crosses of the tenth and later centuries and appears on slabs perhaps as early as the eighth century.[3] It is commonly assumed that the ultimate origin of the type is the early Christian *chrism* or Chi-Ro monogram; that this had a direct bearing on the cross-heads with the arms confined within the circle is perhaps admissible, but there is too great a chronological gap between the chrism and the late wheel-head form, with the arms extending beyond the circle, to render any close connexion at all probable.

The second Scandinavian type of ornament is called the Ringerike style, from the south Norwegian quarry whence came the material for some of its best-known examples. Its distinguishing feature is a treatment of leaf-ornament which Brøndsted convincingly derives from the acanthus ornament of the Winchester School of manuscripts. This foliage, which is seldom combined with animal-forms, has a character of its own, and has discarded the more florid serrations of the true acanthus, elongating the terminal leaf-lobes into long finger-like projections with a little volute at the end of each. At the same time the conventional binding of the Winchester acanthus is often retained to form a centre-

---

[1] *Roy. Com. on Hist. Mons. (Wales), Denbighshire*, p. 159.

[2] Besides the two examples cited the same form occurs at Beckermet (Cumberland), Corwen (Merioneth), Llantysilio yn Ial (Denbigh), Stapleford (Notts.), Fernilee Hall (Derby), Leek (Staffs.), &c.

[3] E.g. the Cuindless slab at Clonmacnois which perhaps commemorates the abbot of that name who died in 720.

PLATE 55

DEERHURST, GLOUCESTERSHIRE, FONT AND
(?) PART OF CROSS-SHAFT
late 9th century

PLATE 56

THE WALLINGFORD SWORD
late 9th century. Ashmolean Museum

point for the design. The two types may be seen in close combination in a drawing (Fig. 42) on one of the terminal leaves of the Caedmon MS.[1] The Ringerike style is safely dated in Scandinavia to the first half of the eleventh century, and the Caedmon MS. is with great probability assigned to the same period.[2]

The English examples (Pl. 58 b) of this style in stone-carving are widely scattered but infrequent.[3] They extend

FIG. 42. Ornaments from the Caedmon MS., c. 1030.

from Great Canfield in Essex to Bibury (Fig. 43) in Gloucestershire, and generally diverge from their Scandinavian originals in including animal-forms. In an architectural setting the voluted lobes, so characteristic of the style, appear on a capital in the tower of Sompting church, but two more remarkable instances of its architectural use are the carved tympanum at Hoveringham (Notts.) and

[1] *The Caedmon Manuscript*, British Academy, 1927, on fo. 225. On the last leaf of the manuscript are two designs for buckles (?) in the same style.

[2] By the named drawing of Alfwine, who is reasonably identified with Alfwine who became abbot of Newminster (Winchester) in 1035. The adoption by the miniaturist of the current style of the stone-carver is significant. The two types may also be seen, in a debased form, on the two capitals of the chancel-arch at Bibury, the capital on the north being perhaps inspired by the well-known slabs, with Ringerike ornaments, from this church, now in the British Museum.

[3] See the list compiled by Reginald Smith in *Proc. Soc. Antiq.*, xxvi, p. 71, to which must be added the stone at Great Canfield, Essex (*Roy. Com. on Hist. Mons., Essex*, iv, p. xxxi).

the lintel at Southwell Cathedral (Pl. 59 *a*). These examples may perhaps date from after the Conquest, though
the lintel is re-used in an early twelfth-century building;
both represent the conflict between St. Michael and the
dragon, the archangel bearing, in one instance, the kite-
shaped shield. The foli-
age which wreaths the
dragon is, however, still
distinctive, and the whole
composition may serve
as yet another instance
of the Saxo-Norman
overlap and incidentally
of the superiority of the
native carver over his
Norman supplanter.
Another tympanum at
Knook (Wilts.) illustrates
the close connexion often
existing between manu-
script and sculptural de-
coration. Fig. 44 shows
three examples, side by
side, the first in manu-
script, of the early part
of the eleventh century, the second in stone, of perhaps
the middle of the same century, and the last in wood, a
twelfth-century Icelandic copy of English work.

FIG. 43.   Bibury, Glos. Tomb-slab, early
eleventh century.

We must now turn to consider the development of later
Saxon figure-sculpture. It has already been shown that
there is reason for assigning the two large figures at Breedon
(Pl. 60) and the companion figure at Castor (Northants.)
to late in the eighth or early in the ninth century. To much
the same period must also be assigned the group including
the smaller figure at Castor, the two at Fletton, and the
figures on the Hedda stone (Pl. 30) at Peterborough

PLATE 57

GOSFORTH, CUMBER-
LAND, CROSS
10th century

WOLVERHAMPTON, STAFFS.,
CROSS-SHAFT
late 10th century

PLATE 58

a. BROMPTON, YORKS., HOG-BACK
late 10th or early 11th century

b. GUILDHALL, LONDON, MEMORIAL STONE,
WITH RINGERIKE ORNAMENT
early 11th century

These two groups together with the figure-sculpture on a number of midland cross-shafts provide a fairly representative collection of Mercian sculpture of the age immediately preceding the Danish invasions. Subsequent to the anarchic period resultant on these incursions and attempts at conquest, the centre of gravity, both political and artistic, of the nation had definitely shifted from Mercia to Wessex, and from henceforth to the Norman Conquest the examples of English figure-sculpture, scattered, scanty, and unrelated as they may appear, are nearly all to be found

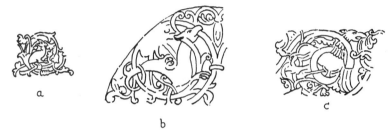

FIG. 44. *a* MS. Aldhelm, Lambeth. *b* Knook, Wilts. *c* Copenhagen Museum.

in the southern counties. Of these examples very few are so placed or so accompanied as to provide evidence of their date, and we are left, very largely, to first principles to set them in any chronological order. A careful analysis, however, of the surviving examples permits certain facts to emerge which are not without significance. The twin-angels (Pl. 60) above the chancel-arch at Bradford-on-Avon group themselves with the angel on the apse at Deerhurst. Both these examples are almost certainly in their original position, and must be contemporary with the buildings on which they are placed. The study of the details of Deerhurst led Prof. Baldwin Brown to place it early in the post-Danish period, and there is much at Bradford indicating a similar date. We may then provisionally place this small group in the first half of the tenth century, in spite of the fact that the veiled hands and the whole attitude of the Bradford angels are so closely paralleled in Ethelwold's Benedictional that a rather later date would seem to be implied. At the end of the period must be placed the two slender figures supporting the defaced sundial on the tower at Langford, which from its architectural detail cannot long have preceded the Norman Conquest.

Other examples are exceedingly difficult to place; thus the bust of Christ in a roundel at Gloucester (Bishop's Palace) is badly defaced, and classification is largely guesswork. The external rood at Romsey (Pl. 61) would seem to be a sophisticated and consequently late example of the Winchester school, while the fully draped rood at Langford (Pl. 61) has been regarded by a distinguished French scholar as a copy of the *Volto Santo* at Lucca, and consequently hardly earlier than the twelfth century. This, we think, is an error; for not only does the Langford rood not display the strong characterization of the Lucca figure, but the rebated jointing of the stones of which it is composed is a definitely pre-Conquest usage. We prefer, therefore, to class it with the draped crucifixes [1] which were general throughout the Christian world from the seventh or eighth to the ninth or tenth century.

Another example, equally difficult to place, is the pair of sculptured panels (Pl. 62) now in the choir at Chichester Cathedral. These have obvious analogies with the carved panels of a Carolingian diptych, and have few points of contact with post-Conquest sculpture. We are therefore justified in assigning them to the late Saxon period, but can hardly attempt to date them more closely. A somewhat similar panel with the Crucifixion survives in

---

[1] The draped crucifix appears to have replaced the undraped form derived from the Hellenistic tradition in the seventh century in Italy. Figures with only the loin-cloth appear on the wooden doors of S. Sabina, Rome (fifth century?), on an ivory in the British Museum (early fifth century), on the Ruthwell cross (late seventh century), and elsewhere, and are implied in Gregory of Tours's account of the crucifix at Narbonne (sixth century). The draped form appears on Theodolinda's crucifix (*c.* 600), in the catacombs of St. Valentine, Rome (seventh century), and thence onwards. See E. Mâle, *L'art religieux du* XIIe *siècle en France*, pp. 78–9.

PLATE 59

a. SOUTHWELL CATHEDRAL, CARVED LINTEL IN N. TRANSEPT
mid 11th century

b. HOVERINGHAM, NOTTS., CARVED TYMPANUM
mid 11th century

PLATE 60

BREEDON, LEICESTERSHIRE, ANGEL
late 8th century

BRADFORD-ON-AVON, WILTS., ANGEL
early 10th century

the church of St. Dunstan, Stepney (Pl. 62). Finally we
must draw attention to a piece of sculpture of quite unusual excellence: the Virgin and Child at York Minster
(Pl. 63). The main argument for placing it in the pre-
Conquest period is its entire dissimilarity from any English
work of post-Conquest age. It occupies, however, a similar
position of isolation in the alternative period, and this
argument therefore carries no conviction. The relief is
characterized by an entire mastery of material, by an
assurance in pose and a sophistication in drapery which
in style and feeling belong to the renaissance of Byzantine
art under the Macedonian emperors. In the museum at
Constantinople is a figure of the Virgin (found in 1922)
which bears a striking resemblance both in character and
execution to the figure at York. This Byzantine figure is
dated by Diehl [1] to the tenth century, and is paralleled by
a number of other sculptures of the same epoch and provenance. That this school of sculpture extended into Italy [2]
and perhaps Germany is proved by its surviving remains,
but what influence it can have had on English work of the
same or a succeeding period is difficult to determine.

There are traces in several English churches of a plastic
decoration of the wall-surface above the chancel-arch,
partly executed in stone and partly in some other material,
perhaps stucco. [3] Thus the angels at Bradford-on-Avon obviously require a central crucifix to complete the composition; at Bibury and Deerhurst are stone panels, the former
retaining remains of carving but the latter now cut back
flush with the wall; and finally at Barton-on-Humber there
is a carved head above the chancel-arch, perhaps also part

[1] C. Diehl, *Manuel d'art byzantin*, 2nd ed., ii, p. 653.
[2] E. g. a Virgin in S. Maria in Porto, Ravenna (*ibid.*, ii, p. 654), a Virgin and
Child in S. Maria in Gradi, Arezzo, dated by G. Franciosi to 1050 (*Arezzo*,
pp. 30 and 34), and a Virgin in stucco at Gernrode, illustrated in M. Sauer-
landt, *Deutsche Plastik des Mittelalters*.
[3] Fragments of modelled and painted decoration in stucco, of this period, were
found in the excavation of the Saxon church at Glastonbury in 1928.

of a larger composition. Two complete, but much defaced, examples of a similar composition, in stone, survive at Headbourne Worthy and Breamore (Hants), over the west and south doors, respectively; in both cases the Rood is accompanied by figures of the Virgin and St. John.[1]

Side by side with the major examples of sculpture there appears to have also existed a rustic art which is represented by a number of rude, ill-formed, and worse-executed figures, scattered in certain remote churches of the midlands and the south. It will suffice here to mention the examples at Inglesham and Daglingworth without further pursuing a subject which has little significance.

It will thus be seen that the figure-sculpture of the late Saxon period admits, at present, of little or no classification, and still less of any attempt at a chronological scheme. Further study of the subject will, however, no doubt reveal other sculptures of the same age, which at present hide themselves under twelfth-century labels or are still used as building material; and with a greater array of examples it is reasonable to hope that the course and history of this obscure art will one day become more apparent.

There can be little doubt that the great majority of the surviving cross-shafts of the later Saxon periods served as headstones; they are seldom on the scale of the great shafts of the earlier age, and not infrequently bore memorial inscriptions. The form of sepulchral memorial which, however, is most distinctive of the period is the coped (Pl. 64) or gabled tomb-slab. In the north this generally took the particular form known as the 'hog-back' (Pl. 58a), a mass of stone with steeply sloping sides and cambered ridge and finished at each end with the fore-quarters of a bear, whose muzzle receives the ridge of the gable. This use of the animal-form is a direct borrowing from Scandinavia, where it is well exemplified on the richly

---

[1] For illustrations of Headbourne Worthy see *V. C. H., Hants*, iv, facing p. 422, and *Arch. Aeliana*, N.S. i, p. 174.

ornamented collar-harnesses from Jutland and Fyen. The beast-head, derived from the same source, also makes its appearance as an architectural ornament in the south and can be seen in the isolated heads on the church at Deerhurst. The coped slab is not so common in the south, though rich examples occur at Ramsbury and Bexhill (Sussex) (Pl. 64), but the numerous examples of the flat slab, with late ornament, in the Saxon cemetery of Peterborough Abbey, would seem to imply that this form was the more normal. A single headstone, with a rounded head and an inscription to a certain Frithburga, survives at Whitchurch (Hants). It dates, probably, from early in the post-Danish period and has a bust of Christ on one side and a very debased vine-scroll on the other.[1]

But little information has survived concerning the furniture and fittings of the late Saxon churches, and not a single recognizable fragment except in metal is now extant. The few literary references enable us to infer that the greater churches were furnished with the same luxury as their continental contemporaries. Thus at Ely we learn that Abbot Brithnod (died 981) made four wooden statues of Virgins enriched with gold and silver and precious stones, and placed them in pairs on either side of the altar;[2] and again, to satisfy the demands of William the Conqueror,[3] the same convent melted down or sold almost all the gold and silver objects in the church, including 'crosses, altars, shrines, tissues, chalices, patens, basins, buckets, fistulas, goblets, dishes, and above all the figure of St. Mary with the Child seated on a throne of wonderful workmanship which Abbot Elsin (died 1016) had made', and the images of the Virgins mentioned above. It is unnecessary to multiply quotations of this nature, for while they convey a general impression of prodigal expenditure on the ornaments of the churches they supply little information as to their character.

[1] *Hants Field Club*, iv, p. 171.   [2] *Acta Sanctorum* (June), v, p. 449.
[3] *Ibid.*, p. 453.

The ritual arrangements of Canterbury Cathedral at the close of the Saxon period have already been described on a previous page. They show how largely the form of such things had been retained from the usage of the early church, and we will conclude this section with a quotation which will show how this early arrangement was already passing to give place to the ritual divisions of the full Middle Age. Aldred, Archbishop of York (1060–9), added a new presbytery to the church at Beverley,[1] and 'above the choir-door he also caused to be made a *pulpitum* of incomparable work of bronze and gold and silver, and on either side of the loft he set up arches, and in the middle, above the loft, a higher arch, carrying on its top a cross likewise of bronze and gold and silver, skilfully fashioned of Teutonic work'. This is one of the earliest, if not the earliest, reference to the solid screen or *pulpitum* which throughout the later Middle Ages closed in the choir of the monks or canons from the nave.

[1] *Historians of the Church of York* (Rolls Ser.), ii, p. 354; translation by Sir W. St. John Hope, *Archaeologia*, lxviii, p. 51.

PLATE 61

LANGFORD, OXON., ROOD IN PORCH
10th century

ROMSEY, HANTS, ROOD IN CLOISTER
early 11th century

PLATE 62

CHICHESTER CATHEDRAL, PANEL
early 11th century

STEPNEY, MIDDLESEX, CRUCIFIXION
early 11th century

Chapter VII

SPECIAL TYPES OF BUILDING

TWO special types of building, (*a*) the centrally planned church and (*b*) the crypt, both derived from an earlier tradition and both occurring sporadically throughout the Saxon period, will be most conveniently dealt with as a type and not as isolated examples of the period to which they may belong.

The Centrally Planned Church

The centrally planned building forms, for the architect, one of the most attractive essays in his art. Its form admits of almost infinite variety, and its use has been as varied as its form. Architects of almost all ages have experimented with it, but since its beauty is largely confined to its plan and internal effect, it is only occasionally that they have succeeded in procuring for it a fair proportion of popular favour. It is, furthermore, except in its simplest forms, essentially adapted for a domed building, whose great thrust and weight should properly be supported by symmetrically disposed abutments.

Roman Imperial building provides several examples of the form, such as the so-called temple of Minerva Medica and a hall in Hadrian's Villa at Tivoli; but if we follow Strzygowski's argument all these are but borrowings from the Near East. This question of origins need not, however, detain us, as it is only with the form in its Christian application that we have to deal. The churches of Constantine included five which may be assigned to this class: the churches of the Anastasis and the Ascension at Jerusalem;[1] the church of St. Peter at Antioch; the first Lateran baptistery and the Mausoleum of S. Costanza at Rome.[2] Of these, all but the

[1] See plans of the two Jerusalem churches in PP. Vincent and Abel, *Jerusalem.*
[2] See plan as originally designed in C. Cecchelli, *S. Agnese fuori le mura e S. Costanza.*

church at Antioch were primarily designed for other purposes than the ordinary celebration of divine service; two of
them were tomb-chapels, one was built to enshrine a holy
place, and the fourth was a baptistery. This allocation represents fairly accurately the subsequent use of the form in early
Christian architecture. Throughout its early history in the
West the centrally planned church was normally used either
as a tomb-chapel or as a baptistery,[1] and only occasionally
as a church. The most elaborate and beautiful church of
the centrally planned type, built in Italy in the earlier Christian centuries, was S. Vitale of Ravenna,[2] begun in 526;
both in plan and decoration it is essentially Byzantine, and
its complexity is such that it hardly gave rise to any com-
parable work in the West until the Renaissance. While, however, any near copy was beyond the abilities of the Western
peoples in these early ages, S. Vitale and other churches
of simpler plan, such as the two baptisteries of Ravenna,
S. Stefano Rotondo, S. Costanza, and the Lateran baptistery
at Rome and S. Sophia Benevento, may well have inspired
early imitators in both Gaul and England. In Gaul the
form is now only represented by a few baptisteries, such as
Riéz, Fréjus, and perhaps Aix-en-Provence, which date from
the fifth or sixth century, and it is not until Carolingian and
later times that they became at all numerous.

Of the earliest church of this type in England there
remains only a twelfth-century description. This was the
church of St. Mary built at Hexham by St. Wilfrid in the
early years of the eighth century. It is described [3] by Prior
Richard as being in the form of a tower, nearly round and

---

[1] A very elaborate fifth-century baptistery of this type, with a double colonnade,
has recently been excavated at Butrinto (Albania).

[2] See plan showing excavations of atrium in D. Maioli, *Tempio di S. Vitale*,
1903. A very similar arrangement of internal bays and piers was reproduced in
the church of S. Gregory at Etschmiadsin (Armenia), built by the Katholikos
Narses III (640–61). See J. Strzygowski, *Der Dom zu Aachen und seine Entstellung*,
1904.

[3] '(Ecclesia) mirandi operis, et scilicet in modum turris erecta et fere rotunda,
a quatuor partibus totidem porticus habens.' Raine, *Hexham*, 1, 14.

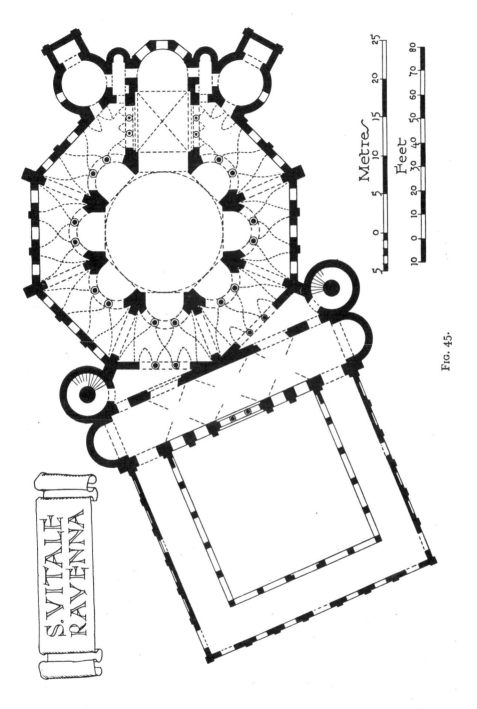

FIG. 45.

S. VITALE
RAVENNA

Metres

Feet

817152

U

with a porticus projecting from each of the four sides. From this we may perhaps infer something in the nature of the Baptistery [1] of the Arians at Ravenna, with or more probably without its ambulatory. The church of St. Mary stood to the south-east of Wilfrid's greater church and is now built

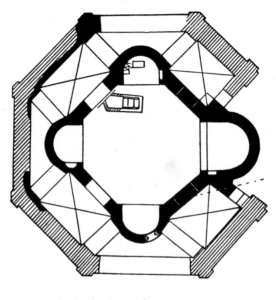

FIG. 46. Arian Baptistery, Ravenna.

over, the houses incorporating portions of the late medieval arcades of a subsequent church.

An entirely new impulse was given to the building of centrally planned churches in the west by the construction of Charlemagne's palace-chapel and mausoleum at Aachen.[2] This structure, which was a remote and barbarous copy of S. Vitale at Ravenna, was octagonal in plan with an

[1] Plan in C. Ricci, *Romanesque Architecture in Italy*, p. vii.
[2] See J. Strzygowski, *Der Dom zu Aachen u. seine Entstellung* (1904); A. Haupt, *Die Pfalzkapelle Karls d. Gr. zu Aachen* (1913); P. Clemen, 'Fouilles et explorations dans l'enceinte du palais impérial carolingien et de la cathédrale d'Aix-la-Chapelle', in *Revue de l'art chrétien*, lxii (1912), pp. 213–20, and *Bau u. Kunstdenkmäler der Rheinprovinz*, x.

PLATE 63

YORK MINSTER, VIRGIN AND CHILD

11th century

PLATE 64

a. DURHAM, CHAPTER-HOUSE, TOMB-SLAB
early 11th century

b. BEXHILL, SUSSEX, TOMB-SLAB
early 11th century

arcade and ambulatory round, a projecting chancel on the east, two staircase towers and a porch on the west, and a large atrium beyond them. It is difficult to understand the impression which this very mediocre building made upon the imagination of western Europe for some centuries after its erection; it is, however, a fact that even after the Con-

AACHEN

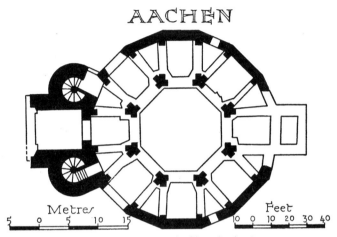

Metres   Feet

FIG. 47. Charlemagne's Church, Aachen.

quest a building was raised at Hereford after the manner of Charlemagne's church at Aachen.

The earliest centrally planned church in England after the Carolingian revival did not follow this model. Alfred's church at Athelney, built late in the ninth century, is described by William of Malmesbury [1] as being 'in a new fashion with four *postes*, planted in the earth to uphold the whole structure, and four *cancelli*, of round form, leading out of the ambulatory'. Except for the uncertainty as to whether the term *postes* implies posts or piers, and consequently whether the building was of timber or stone, the description exactly applies to an early Carolingian building which has fortunately survived in form if not in substance

[1] William of Malmesbury, *De Gestis Pontificum* (Rolls Ser.), p. 199. 'Quattuor enim postes solo infixi totam suspendunt machinam, quattuor cancellis opere sperico in circuitu ductis.'

to the present day. The church of Germigny-des-Prés,[1] near Orléans, was founded by Theodulph, Bishop of Orléans and Abbot of Fleury, about 810, and there can be little doubt that it is the direct ancestor of Alfred's church at Athelney. This form cannot, however, be considered as a Carolingian invention; for while it appears also in the church of S. Satiro at Milan [2] at that period, it is exactly paralleled by the earlier Patriarchal church at Etschmiadsin in Armenia.[3] One must therefore assume that the type was introduced from the East probably by way of Constantinople.

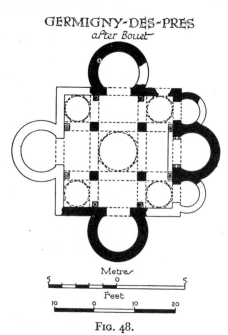

GERMIGNY-DES-PRES
after Bouet

Metre
Feet

FIG. 48.

Later Saxon churches of the centrally planned type appear most commonly to have followed the model of Charlemagne's minster at Aachen. Thus about 960 Abbot Ethelwold built at Abingdon a church which is described in the chronicle [4] as having a round chancel, a round church (or nave) of twice the length of the chancel and a round tower. Some small remains of the chancel of this church or more probably of the crypt beneath it

[1] G. Bouet, 'L'église de Germigny-des-Prés', in *Bulletin Monumental* (1868), p. 566. The inscription on the monument giving the date 806 has been proved fraudulent. See *Bull. Arch.* (1923).

[2] See plan in R. Cattaneo, *Architecture in Italy from the Sixth to the Eleventh Century*, p. 254; it was built in 879.

[3] J. Strzygowski, *Der Dom zu Aachen und seine Entstellung* (1904).

[4] *Chronicon Monasterii de Abingdon* (Rolls Ser.), ii, p. 277: 'Cancellus rotundus erat, ecclesia et rotunda duplicem habens longitudinem quam cancellus; turris quoque rotunda erat.'

were discovered in the excavations of a few years ago. They lay immediately on the axis of the later church and included part of an apsidal east end. The position of the tower is uncertain; it may have formed the central superstructure of the round nave, as Sir Wm. Hope surmised, or it may have stood at the west end like the two staircase towers at Aachen.

Probably about the same time, and in any case in the same tenth century, a circular tomb-chapel was built at Bury St. Edmunds to contain the body of the martyred king. Its remains were discovered when the Lady Chapel was built in 1275, and are described as follows: 'Under the ground were found the walls of an ancient round church, which was much broader than the chapel (this was some 45 ft. wide) and so built that the altar of the chapel was almost in the middle; it was believed that this was the first building constructed in honour of St. Edmund.' [1] The site and some remains of the Lady Chapel of 1275 can still be exactly located, and the expenditure of a few pounds would, no doubt, reveal the remains of its tenth-century predecessor.

It is not necessary to do more than mention the baptistery added to the east of and almost touching his cathedral by Archbishop Cuthbert of Canterbury (741–58). Nothing is known of its form and this [2] is the only record of its existence.

The last and, in some ways, the most interesting of this type of pre-Conquest building was the great rotunda begun but not completed by Abbot Wulfric (1047–59) at St. Augustine's, Canterbury. After the abbot's visit to the Pope at Reims in 1047, he is stated to have begun his scheme for uniting the two early churches of SS. Peter and Paul and St. Mary by pulling down the east end of one and the west

[1] *John of Oxenede's Chronicle* (Rolls Ser.), p. 246: 'sub terra inventi fuerunt muri cujusdam veteris ecclesiae rotundae, quae quidem multo latior fuit quam capella, et ita constructa quod altare capellae quasi in medio ejus fuerat, et creditur illam fuisse ad opus S. Aedmundi primo fuit constructa.'
[2] Edmer, Vita Bregwini, *Anglia Sacra*, ii, p. 186.

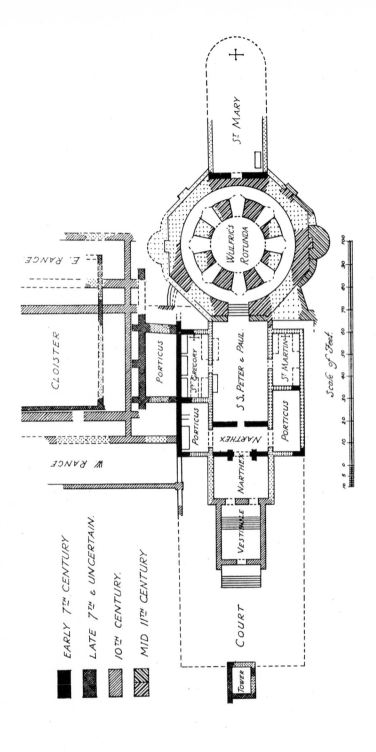

EARLY 7TH CENTURY
LATE 7TH & UNCERTAIN.
10TH CENTURY.
MID 11TH CENTURY

ST MARY

E. RANGE

CLOISTER

WULFRIC'S ROTUNDA

W. RANGE

PORTICUS

ST GREGORY

PORTICUS

S.S. PETER & PAUL

ST MARTIN

NARTHEX

PORTICUS

VESTIBULE

NARTHEX

COURT

TOWER

Scale of Feet.

ST AUGUSTINE'S ABBEY   CANTERBURY

FIG. 49.

end of the other and erecting on the space between them the lower part of the rotunda, of which the remains have been found in the excavations of the last twenty years.[1] At Wulfric's death the building was left incomplete and it was still in that state when the general rebuilding of Abbot Scotland (1070–87) destroyed all that existed above ground. The remains exposed by the excavations showed that the building (Pl. 32 b) was octagonal without and round within, and had an inner circle of eight massive piers of masonry. In the course of the building the outer walls had been thickened and massive towers of semicircular form added on the south and probably also on the north side. That this building was in the nature of a crypt is indicated by the fact that its chalk flooring is some $2\frac{3}{4}$ ft. below the level of that of the adjoining church of SS. Peter and Paul, from which it was approached by a wide doorway and stairs on the axial line of the two buildings. The building throughout is of rubble and is set out with remarkable care and exactitude.

There is some evidence that Wulfric's scheme included the entire rebuilding of the church of SS. Peter and Paul, on a larger scale, but of this work a beginning only was made on the south side.

There can be little doubt that the rotunda was, in some sort, a copy of the more elaborate building erected by St. William of Volpiano at S. Benigne at Dijon in 1011–18. The Dijon building differs only in possessing two rings of columns, otherwise in position and arrangement it is very similar. The two projecting towers, to the north and south, contained staircases, and the lowest stage formed a crypt, the central space, however, being open from the floor to the roof. Unlike France, in England this type of structure found no imitators, and was considered by the late eleventh-century writer Goscelin, trained in the Norman school, as quite unsuited to a monastic building. It is, however, a

---

[1] See Sir W. St. John Hope in *Archaeologia*, lxvi, p. 377, and C. R. Peers and A. W. Clapham in *ibid.*, lxxvii, p. 201.

final illustration of the greater cosmopolitanism of Saxon architecture as compared to the more competent but

FIG. 50. S. Benigne, Dijon.

.equally more restricted and traditional architecture of the Normans.

Crypts

The origin of the use of crypts in Christian churches must without doubt be derived from the subterranean chambers in the Roman and other catacombs which contained the tomb of some well-known saint. The catacombs of course were grouped along and under the roads leading away from the city and were all outside the walls. The chaotic political condition of Italy in the seventh and eighth centuries rendered at times the visit to these suburban cemeteries an undertaking of some danger, and as a consequence we find in the eighth century the beginning of the practice of transferring the bodies of the saints from their original resting-place to specially prepared crypts beneath the intramural churches. It is not, however, to be supposed that these eighth-century crypts, constructed generally beneath the high altar of the church, were the first of their kind. Already great suburban churches had been built above the tombs of the most important apostles and saints, and the tomb-crypts or *confessios* at St. Peter's, St. Paul without the Walls, and St. Stephen on the Latin Way were no doubt of far earlier date. The origin of the two classes, however, was essentially different, in that in one the crypt was constructed under a pre-existing church, and in the other a church was constructed over a pre-existing tomb. The early crypts themselves show evident traces of their typological origin in the catacombs; they normally consist of a central tomb-chamber, approached and often surrounded by one or more narrow galleries, an evident attempt to reproduce the circumstances of the primitive burial-place.

According to Corrado Ricci,[1] the earliest datable example of a *confessio* constructed under a church is that at S. Crisogono, Rome, built at any rate as early as *c.* 730. It was followed by those at S. Cecilia (817–24), S. Marco (827–44), and S. Apollinare Nuovo, Ravenna (eighth and ninth century). The plan of all these is similar, consisting of a central tomb-chamber under the altar with a circular gallery round it following the curve of the apse. The tomb-chamber commonly had an opening in the west wall from

---

[1] C. Ricci, *Romanesque Architecture in Italy*, p. viii.

which the tomb itself could be seen from the church, for the crypt was not wholly sunk below the floor-level.

Comparatively few crypts of this early type have been entirely preserved outside Italy. In France the most remarkable is that under the church of S. Aphrodise at Béziers.[1] This consists of the central tomb-chamber with its surrounding gallery and opening in the west wall; it is built in 'petit appareil' and may well date from Merovingian times. Curiously enough two English crypts of this type are safely dated to the last quarter of the seventh century, and are thus earlier than any datable example in Italy. It must thus be assumed that they are copied from one or other of the Roman suburban churches, probably St. Peter's, of which the plan, as it was in the sixteenth century, is preserved in a drawing by Benedetto Drei.[2] Nearly all the later Saxon crypts are based on the same plan with more or less modification, and as all of them present some feature of interest it will be necessary to consider each in turn.

(a) *Hexham.* This is definitely referred to in Eddius' contemporary description [3] of Wilfrid's church at Hexham and may thus be assigned to *c.* 675. It lies under the east end of the existing nave, and the discoveries referred to on p. 45 show that it can never have been under the high altar of the church. This, as we have seen, is the normal position for the *confessio*, but the church of St. Stephen on the Latin Way, at Rome, provides a parallel to the position of the crypt at Hexham. The building itself (Pl. 65) consists of a central chamber with a vestibule on the west, and three galleries of access, two towards the east and one towards the west. The structure would appear to have been entirely underground, as there is no provision for the usual window-opening in the west wall. The walls are

---

[1] Coste, *S. Aphrodise et son Église* (1899).
[2] De Rossi, *Inscrip. christ.* ii, p. 235.
[3] Eddius, *Vita Wilfridi*, chap. xxii: 'domum Domino . . . fundavit, cujus profunditatem in terra cum domibus mire politis lapidibus fundatam, etc.'

PLATE 65

HEXHAM, NORTHUMBERLAND, CRYPT LOOKING W.
late 7th century

built of re-used Roman masonry, and the main chamber
and vestibule are roofed with a barrel-vault. The passages
are roofed with slabs and there are several lamp-niches in
the walls.

(b) *Ripon.* The documentary evidence for the date of the

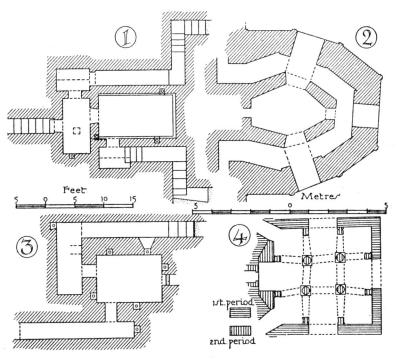

FIG. 51. Crypts. 1. Hexham; 2. Wing; 3. Ripon; 4. Repton.

crypt at Ripon is not so strong as at Hexham, Eddius merely
recording that the church was built of ashlar 'from the
foundations in the earth' up to the summit of the structure.
The building, however, is so similar to that at Hexham that
there can be no doubt as to its being Wilfrid's work. Here
again the crypt consists of a main chamber and a vestibule
to the west, but the galleries of access are less elaborate and
are reduced to two, one opening to the east and one to the
west. The walls are of local ashlar, cut for the purpose, the
main chamber has a barrel-vault and the vestibule a half

barrel-vault butting against the east wall. The position of the Ripon crypt in relation to the early church above it is quite unknown.

(c) *Brixworth*. The apsidal sanctuary of the seventh-century church at Brixworth is surrounded on the outside of the wall by a semi-subterranean gallery formerly roofed with a barrel-vault. It was approached by two doors flanking the arch of the sanctuary, and was undoubtedly planned in connexion with a central chamber under the apse itself. Whether this chamber was ever constructed is doubtful as excavation has revealed no trace of its existence. In the outer wall of the gallery are two arched recesses, perhaps intended for the reception of sarcophagi.

The three crypts described above are the only ones which survive of the early Saxon period. The remaining examples all belong to the later or Carolingian period and indicate some slight elaboration of the earlier plan. In addition to the existing crypts, reference should here be made to the documentary evidence for similar structures at Canterbury and Winchester cathedrals cited above (pp. 86 and 87).

(d) *Wing*. Under the apsidal chancel of Wing church is an irregularly planned crypt consisting of a central chamber of elongated octagonal form, with a window-opening in the west wall and three arches opening into the surrounding gallery. This gallery is approached from the east end of the two aisles of the nave and has two openings in the outer wall. The whole structure is built of the rudest rubble masonry with barrel-vaulting in the same material.

(e) *Abingdon*. The excavations of 1921–2 at Abingdon Abbey revealed only one fragment of the church built by Ethelwold *c.* 960. This was part of the apsidal east end, which from its relatively low level and the narrow diameter of the apse seemed to imply the former existence of a central chamber-crypt with encircling gallery. No trace, however, was found of the outer wall. The building was of rough rubble.

(*f*) *Repton.* Under the rectangular chancel of Repton is a crypt of the same form (Frontispiece), roofed with a stone vault supported on four pillars. It seems certain that this vault was added to a pre-existing crypt at a comparatively late date, probably early in the eleventh century. The date or dates of the earlier part of the building are uncertain but may go back to before the Danish invasion. The columns have moulded capitals and a spiral moulding carried up the shafts; from the capitals spring cross-arches and the roof between is a rough vault, sometimes rudely groined. From the three external sides of the crypt project recesses extending beyond the outer walls and enclosed by retaining walls; these would seem to have been lighting areas. In the west wall is a similar recess with a window opening towards the nave of the church.

(*g*) *Sidbury.* Under the Norman chancel at Sidbury (Devon) is a small rectangular crypt, of which the walls do not align with those of the chancel above and which was filled in when the chancel was built. It was approached by a western staircase in the north-west angle and retains no trace of a stone vault.

(*h*) *Glastonbury.* An eighth crypt, of a rather different type, has recently been added to the list by the excavations in the nave of Glastonbury Abbey in the summer of 1928. It appears probable that this tiny building (13 ft. by $5\frac{1}{2}$ ft. internally) originally stood isolated in the cemetery, forming a small mausoleum partly below and partly above ground. It was approached by a flight of steps at the west end and bore a striking resemblance, both in plan and structure, to the 'Hypogeum of the Martyrs' outside the town of Poitiers.[1] The date of the building at Glastonbury is uncertain, but it seems quite clear that it is more ancient than the chancel of Dunstan's church, which was built around and above it about the middle of the tenth century.

[1] C. de la Croix, *Hypogée Martyrium de Poitiers.*

The original purpose of Wilfrid's crypts seems almost certainly to have been the housing of relics of the saints that he brought from Rome, and Ailred of Rievaulx records that Eilaf removed the sacred remains from the underground place and enshrined them behind the high altar. That they were not in the early period used for

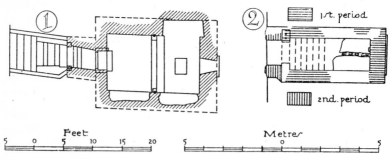

FIG. 52.   Crypts.   1. Poitiers; 2. Glastonbury.

burial is proved by the fact that neither Wilfrid nor Acca his successor was buried in the crypt at Ripon or Hexham. Some of the crypts of the later churches, however, seem certainly to have served this purpose. Several bishops of Winchester were buried in the crypt there, and it seems not improbable that the main purpose of Wulfric's rotunda-crypt at Canterbury was the more honourable entombment of the bodies of the early archbishops and members of the house of Ethelbert which were the chief treasure of the monastery.

INDEX